T0170410

Hoodoo in the Psalms

God's Magick

Hoodoo in the Psalms

God's Magick

Taren S

MOON
BOOKS

Winchester, UK
Washington, USA

JOHN HUNT PUBLISHING

First published by Moon Books, 2019
Moon Books is an imprint of John Hunt Publishing Ltd., No. 3 East Street, Alresford
Hampshire SO24 9EE, UK
office@jhpbooks.com
www.johnhuntpublishing.com
www.moon-books.net

For distributor details and how to order please visit the 'Ordering' section on our website.

Text copyright: Taren S 2018

ISBN: 978 1 78904 206 1
978 1 78904 207 8 (ebook)
Library of Congress Control Number: 2018956752

All rights reserved. Except for brief quotations in critical articles or reviews, no part of this
book may be reproduced in any manner without prior written permission from the publishers.

The rights of Taren S as author have been asserted in accordance with the Copyright, Designs
and Patents Act 1988.

A CIP catalogue record for this book is available from the British Library.

Design: Stuart Davies

UK: Printed and bound by CPI Group (UK) Ltd, Croydon, CR0 4YY
US: Printed and bound by Thomson-Shore, 7300 West Joy Road, Dexter, MI 48130

We operate a distinctive and ethical publishing philosophy in
all areas of our business, from our global network of authors to
production and worldwide distribution.

Contents

Psalm 54 - Destroying one's enemies
Psalm 55 - Dividing your enemies
Psalm 59 & 83 - Asking God to judge your enemies
Psalm 94 - Stopping a bitter enemy
Psalm 110 - Confusing your enemies
Psalm 125 - Keeping enemies from harming you
Psalm 7 - Stopping a curse or hex
Psalm 35 - Returning a curse to sender
Psalm 109 - Cursing someone who has wronged you
Psalm 109 - Stopping someone from doing evil against you
Psalm 71 - Breaking up with a cruel man/woman
Psalm 51 - Self protection
Psalm 89 & 91 - Protection

6. Legal-Justice-Jail   107
Psalm 7 - Justice in Court/legal matters
Psalm 26 - Staying out of jail
Psalm 46 - Uniting disagreeing parties/stop quarreling
Psalm 94 - Being falsely accused
Psalm 99 - Justice in legal matters
Psalm 119 - Wrongful persecution
Psalm 119 - Appearing before a Judge
Psalm 142 - Seeking early release from prison
Psalm 142 - Protection from the law

7. Prophecy-Influencing Others-Dreams   117
Psalm 49 - Gaining the second sight-prophecy
Psalm 78 - Increasing psychic abilities
Psalm 114 - Influencing others with your thoughts
Psalm 64 - Stopping someone from telling your secrets
Psalm 70 - Stopping someone from working against you
Psalm 119 - Needing others to accomplish a goal
Psalm 119 - Wanting people to agree with you
Psalm 130 - Seeking aid from others

Dedicated

To all my
Moon sisters & brothers

To those that seek truths

Introduction

Part 1 Hoodoo

This ain't no fancy man's magick, this is real folks just doin' what needed done.

Hoodoo is the working folk's magickal realm. We use what we have. We use what we need. It's about finding a parking space, stopping a neighbor from gossiping about you, helping to insure your luck is good at Friday's bingo game, clearing obstacles in your path. We are not trying to turn lead into gold, just attract the gold to us.

Hoodoo references 'workings' instead of spells or incantations. It is a very positive approach to any magick done. It is a working. It worked. No room for doubt or failure. Hoodoo folk 'practice' nothing, that doesn't get the job done. A working does.

The magick of Hoodoo is regional, cultural, and very personal. The land you stand on determines the magick you use. Your personal story determines the magick you use. How it all makes you feel determines the magick you use. Therefore, we have so many different methods, ways, opinions, etc. regarding the magick in Hoodoo.

Through the blended magickal knowledge, of both immigrant and slave folks, Hoodoo became the name for the magick that was developed throughout the Southeastern region of America. Based within very ancient magickal knowledge and then infused with the energies of the different folks' native magick and the land they now stood upon, a very powerful magickal system developed.

In plain speak, "folks be sharing what they know". When the first boat of European folks landed on Plymouth Rock, they brought their beliefs and their magick. The Native American folks already living there had some magick, then the African and Caribbean folks' magick was added. The guiding factor in all of this was absolute faith and belief in Divinity. They didn't worry what name you called Divinity, just so longed as you had faith and belief in it.

Hoodoo is where the country folk are. The good, hardworking folk that seem to blend into countryside. The ones closest to the land, the energies of the seasons, and the coming storms. With this connection, through unspoken faith, they know magick is a part of everything.

Upon reflection, you realize most country or rural type folks all over the world, who are doing magick connected to the land and to Divinity are doing Hoodoo. It is not just a southern thing. That just happens to be where it was named.

Hoodoo is and isn't many things. Defining it so that it fits to every regional, cultural and personal adaption is, well, impossible. The prayer lady in Tennessee never compared notes with the Georgia healer. The Gullah conjurers have no connection to the New Orleans practitioners. Alabama swamp folk have a different story than the North Carolina Mountain folk. What they all do have in common is that they learned to connect to the spark of Divinity that is within them. The same spark that is within you. That is within me. It is within us all.

Prayer healing or faith healing has been used through the ages. In America, among the mountain folks in the southern Appalachian region - Tennessee, Georgia, West Virginia and both Carolinas, this has been used since the immigrants settled there. Through their ancestral history, there are lines of magick that link directly back to the British Isles. A place full of ancient and mystic magickal knowledge. These immigrants used the connection of the new land and their faith to create magick.

Marie Laveau, Bayou John and George W. Cable are all New Orleans famous Hoodoo practitioners. In some parts of southern American, they almost became household names. Not the names you said out loud in well-mannered company, but the ones spoken softly in secret when you had a problem that needed fixing.

New Orleans magickal folks move to the beat of a different drum, which is a polite way of saying, they do things a bit different down there. Not saying nothin' bad, just different. Their magickal roots give them a diverse flavor. They have more of a Caribbean/Jamaican influence with French immigrants bringing Roman Catholicism into the mix. The end result; quite powerful magick that is still sought after today.

The Gullah folks probably have the most interesting story to tell. One of oppression, persecution, murder, injustice and in the end, very powerful magickal conjurers. Talk about making lemonade out of lemons. Well, these folks have earned the right to be highly respected conjurers internationally.

This is a story of the origins of the Gullah folk. The Haitian Voodoo Priest who owns the Botanica I worked at liked to tell the story to anyone who would listen to that sort of thing. He would stand a little taller and speak in that "all knowing" tone. The beginning never changed. "It all started in Haiti with a ship", he would proudly start the story.

Haitian folks have been known to spend an entire afternoon telling just one very long, never ending story. The short version of a long story of his afternoon of chest thumping is still just as interesting. The Gullah folk are descendants of a group of Haitian slaves that revolted on a ship, off the coast of Charleston, SC. Afterwards, they landed on the outer banks, near Beaufort, SC. There they lived, mostly undisturbed by the outside modern world, until the 1950's. In the local area, they developed a reputation as respected magickal folk blending their native beliefs with Protestant Christianity.

The chances are, this is an urban myth told by both Haitians and the local Gullah folks as there is no hard evidence. The documented history states they are descendants from West Africa and Haiti with no mention of a slave ship revolt. Probably, they escaped from one or several of the local plantations and went to the outer banks area of South Carolina. There, they were mostly forgotten until the 1950's when paved roads and interstates linked folks to each other. Either way, it makes for a great story to tell the young ones on a warm southern evening when sipping sweet iced tea. No matter the beginning, in the end there is powerful magick among the Gullah.

While countless myths and stories surround Hoodoo, the ever present magick was and is always respected. Various misunderstandings and Hollywood stories have fueled the dark side of a vibrant and colorful magickal system that at its core always shows respect and reverence for Divinity and the Ancestors.

Christians put Divinity in a box, but Divinity never put itself in a box.

When God gave us His sacred text, the Bible, He also gave us His magick. Now remember God is all-wise, so He was smart enough to put the magick in a place where it could not be easily found. Now if you think about this, that is a very good thing. Would we really want everybody, and I do mean everybody, having access to this type of power? Well thank goodness, God was smart enough to know better.

"Hey Witchery. Whatcha doin?" I looked up from behind the counter to see White Truck entering the shop. Folks that shop in the botanica regularly are given expressive names by the Haitian Priest. She is called White Truck because she drives a white truck and I am called Witchery well, because I practice Hoodoo or Witchcraft, root working, conjuring or the other names whispered in corners about my folks.

It was a typical Low Country summer day, sticky and damn hot. South Carolina has two seasons, hot and not hot. With the temperature up, everybody was at home and the shop empty for a normal, busy afternoon. I was working on another Psalm and quite excited about the depth of magick I was finding when White Truck strolled in.

She was immediately interested in the paperwork I had laid all over the counter in my quest for finding every magickal working verse in the Book of Psalms. And I knew she was interested and that wasn't necessarily a good thing. White Truck came to the shop looking for scraps of magick, which really wasn't hard, it was a botanica or magick shop.

You would think if you hang out long enough at a botanica something is bound to slip by, or up and wham, you now have valuable magickal knowledge that you can use or sell. Or at least, that was White Truck's thinking. I, one time gave her a list of about ten herbs and their magickal uses. I later heard from one of her friends that she had been busy. She used the list to concoct some love spell to try to get a married man she liked to ask her out. Then she tried to sell the stuff to another person, claiming it was her grandmother's recipe.

Half absently, I wondered what she is trying to cook up now. I gathered my papers while giving her a smile and nod. No sense in making enemies if you don't have to. As far as I was concerned, White Truck had re-affirmed a lesson. A very important lesson. Magick is not for everyone.

The magick is hidden for a reason, but the trail to it is quite easy to find if you have faith and belief. Within the Bible there are stories of miracles and magick. Many of us grew up hearing various stories of Jonah in the whale for numerous days, Joshua blowing a horn to bring down city walls, the dead rising, water turning to wine, the burning bush and parting of the seas; the list could go on for pages. Magick is all over the Bible whether the Pastor wants to admit it or not.

If we are wanting to go to the very beginning of this story, then we must look back about 3,000 years or so. God spoke to and through some folks in a village. Those folks became the Jewish tribe. Some of them didn't quite like the way things were being done and they became Christians. Somewhere in all this, folks started writing down words inspired by God and words spoken to God. Those texts became the Old Testament.

Yes, this is a very simple explanation for a very large subject matter. Tracing lines of magick will take us on a journey of over 40,000 years of modern human history. Divinity has been with us since the beginning and so too has magick. To keep this book a readable length, this grimoire's focus is on the magick in the Psalms.

The Books of Psalms are NOT the words of God. They are Man's words To God. First spoken and then later written down, these are the prayers used for asking for God's aid, strength, wisdom, and protection and vengeance. These words were spoken before there were Christians.

Throughout our history, the magick of the Psalms has been used repeatedly. There are documented examples of such use of the Psalms. One notable working is in the ancient city of Pompeii, where an archeologist found a piece of slate with curses written on it, using verses from the Book of Psalms, against the citizens of Pompeii.

One of the oldest known grimoires (book of spells) dates from 1496. Known as the Heptameron, the book contains spells using verses from the Psalms and, at one time, was used throughout Europe; occult historians consider it to be the most powerful spell book of its time. Today, both the magickal and academic community still use and study the Heptameron.

Within Jewish mysticism, the Qabalah has an entire section for the magickal use of the Book of Psalms. Their system teaches that within the Book of Psalms there are different and sacred names of God to be used for a magickal or prayer purpose.

The Psalms contains two types of verses, lamentations and

incantations. Lamentations are sorrows that we give to God. The soul wrenching echoes of women, sobbing upon learning their son or daughter, who was a soldier, will not be returning home are true lamentations. A deep, heartbreaking wail given to God asking for comfort. These words are the lamentation verses within the Psalms; first spoken, then written down so future generations may use them if needed.

The second type of verses within the Psalms are the incantations. The magick of God. Here are the directions for using the preferred herbs, the taking of a ritual bath and the words of magick to be used. Everything you need to know to do the magick of God is in the Psalms. Here lays the path to moving the universe to left or right; to tipping the scales a bit to our side.

Jewish mysticism brings to light that all we need to know to use the Psalms is to understand them. When, what, where, why, and how—they are all answered within the Book of Psalms, waiting for the anointed mind to open its secrets. The lighting of candles; the use of incense and herbal offerings; taking a spiritual bath; petitions; giving thanks, are all there, in the Book of Psalms.

Both Jewish and early Christian mysticism make known the importance of numerology - the use of sacred or holy numbers. Numbers have been given relationships in the magickal use of the Book of Psalms. The most sacred number is 3 - the Holy Trinity, representing the Father, Son & Holy Ghost. 1-3-5-7-9-12 and 21 are most common sacred numbers used in combinations. Using the sacred numbers and the different names/aspect of God in each Psalm make combinations of active verses in a Psalm become powerful workings.

During the Middle Ages the Catholic Church repressed any mystical knowledge within the Bible and destroyed any known magickal manuscripts; copies of Christian magickal books were secreted away with Christian historians and occultists being put to death for even having knowledge of them. The mystical use of the Psalms had to go underground for hundreds of years. It is a testament to those people that the magick survived to be passed to the generations to come.

Somehow, somewhere in the physical, astral and/or spiritual worlds this magickal knowledge was passed to folks standing on a new land. In the early 1800's is when our story begins. That is when there is documented evidence of roots of a strong magickal system in place throughout the southern parts of America. The magick is named Hoodoo. The working man's magick, the everyday folk just doing what needed getting done.

She almost smiled when she opened the door to the shop and saw me sitting behind the counter. Myrtle Beach Lady is her shop name. She is a very knowledgeable practitioner of Low Country Hoodoo with a large clientele base throughout both North and South Carolina. She would say that she only does "Jesus magick", meaning if you can't say "In Jesus's name" at the end of whatever you are doing then she "ain't doing it".

The first year I worked at the shop, she would act like I didn't exist. Completely ignored me. If I asked her a question, she would look the other way, pretending she didn't see or hear me. White girls who practice Witchery are dangerous, she would tell the Haitian Priest with her backed turned to me (like he is not going to tell me everything she said when she leaves the shop). She was sure that I was up to no good, and/or nothing good was going to come of me being there.

Once, she told him I had too much book knowledge and then complained that I didn't know one of the herbs of over 130 jars on the back wall. Or that white girls cried a lot, so he should be careful. He would tell me what she had said, laughing about it and assuring me that MB Lady would like me one day. That day couldn't come soon enough, I thought. All I can think about is her glaring at me.

Things started to turn around when she overheard me speaking with a customer. She liked what she heard and nodded her head. For me, it was like getting a gold star for a job well done. When she left,

I went to find the Haitian Priest in the back of the shop to tell him about my new approval rating. Just maybe, this Witchery wasn't some dumb white girl after all.

She finally had to speak to me when the Haitian Priest was out for the afternoon and I was the only one there to get what she needed in the back of the shop. As usual, I was deep in the Psalms and mumbling about some notes I had made. Most of the regulars at the shop knew I had taken on the task of identifying the active verses in all 150 Psalms and putting them into magickal workings.

"At least she is not glaring at me today", my inside voice said, as I watched her approach the counter.

She looked down at my tablet and handwritten notes and without missing a beat,

"Psalm 91", she quipped.

"The Psalm of Protection", I quickly replied and didn't look up at her.

"Psalm 119?" With an arched eyebrow she asked.

"The longest Psalm with many magickal verses in it." This time I looked up and smiled at her as the words came out.

That started a wonderful conversation lasting over an hour and into years of many other afternoon chats. She told me stories of folks in the Bible doing magick. Just plain, everyday folks doing magick was always the theme. She knows the key to the magick of Divinity is faith and numbers.

Myrtle Beach Lady always works within "holy numbers". Numbers she has found to be magickal, for some reason or another. She is highly secretive of telling folks the numbers because she said that God told her not to tell. My thoughts are she says that so White Truck and similar minded folks leave her alone and stop asking.

Once, I asked her where she learned about magick. Her great auntie taught her about it. I then asked if she knew where auntie learned it.

"Does it matter? Why worry about the past when folks have needs right now?" she shot back to me.

I understand most folks working a 60 hour week and trying to pay bills would agree with her. They would just want the magick to work.

"Maybe we need to keep the links to the past" was my soft-spoken opinion.

"The only link you need to worry about is the one to Divinity", she stated with authority and ending that part of the conversation.

I think the last year or so, MB Lady has been pretending not to approve of me. I saw her almost smile at me as she entered the shop. Helping to keep her ruse, I just keep typing on my tablet.

"Are you done yet? How long have you been working on that book of yours?" she asked while walking toward the counter.

"I don't know, don't have an end date, just enjoying the journey", I responded, smiling warmly at her. She paused for a moment, and then looked me deep in my eyes and smiled back.

"Amen, amen, amen", she said with vibrating, magickal intent, as she lay her hand on my tablet. "This book of yours is going to be published. I just made sure of that."

Time to tell the Haitian Priest my approval rating went up.

Like the beginnings of many stories that over time develop myths, so too has the roots of Hoodoo. All those culturally varied folks, in different parts of a region, tapped into something wonderful, magickal and spiritual. It took the different backgrounds and various cultures, of folks standing in one place together, to realize that Divinity is with each of us, in its own unique way. Our job is to celebrate and use this connection to create a better life.

Combining magickal workings developed and used over a millennium for the modern mystic to use today, this body of work strives to give you the most useful grimoire of the Psalms for the 21st century. From texts long covered in dust, to 19th century Marie Laveau, to the modern-day Doc Buzzard (a famous mid-20th century root man in South Carolina & Georgia), the sum of this magick is about enriching our personal lives and keeping

Divinity close to us.

Some 43 of the workings are about seeking to be a better person and strengthening our relationship with Divinity. Another 37 relate to family, home and health. Another 18 relate to wealth, prosperity and blessings. Within this magickal text also lies the path to "righteous vengeance" and the ability for asking God to judge your enemies. It is measured as an eye for an eye and a tooth for a tooth... Leviticus 24:20. There are 23 workings for this.

Who Wrote The Book of Psalms?

David wrote 73 Psalms. Twelve Psalms bear the name of Asaph, the conductor of David's choir of the temple (1 Chron. 16:7; 2 Chron. 29:30). Asaph's Psalms are Psalm 50 and 73-83. Ten Psalms are written by the sons of Korah (Ps. 42; 44-49; 84; 85; 87), two by Solomon (Ps. 72 and 127), one each by Moses (Ps. 90), Ethan (Ps. 89) and Heman (Ps. 88). The remaining 50 Psalms bear no author's name.

Part 2 You Do

In the beginning….. Through the understanding of faith in Divinity the use of magick developed.

Those are mighty big words. Read them again, aloud. "Through the understanding of faith in Divinity the use of magick developed." Think deep, and hard about those words. Let this knowledge resonate within your soul. The Divine is magick and magick is Divine. So long as we strive to stay in the Light of Divinity, our lives will be blessed.

We need to look within, for that is where the power lays. The power of Divinity is within each, and every one of us. When the universe first came into being, so too came Divinity, and magick. This is a very Pagan creation story that really sums it all up nicely. In the beginning, when that first particle of matter appeared, Divinity and magick were within. As the universe grew, so too did Divinity and magick. This tells us that is all starts within. So where do you think you should be looking for your connection and your magick?

The first step is all about You and your relationship to Divinity. You are a part of Divinity and Divinity is part of you. Here are a few questions to ask yourself. What is the name or image you use to relate to Divinity? Is it God or is it the Goddess? Are there many Gods, or just One?

You must find your connection to Divinity in whatever way that works for you. This is very personal and between you and Divinity. Do what feels right. Listen to that inside voice and believe. Really, it is that simple. Belief and faith in Divinity are the guiding factors of all Hoodoo folk no matter where they may be standing. It is a combination of magick and spiritually.

Hoodoo is a tool that can be used by everyone. Divinity is the One; the All. There is no Holy name(s) given in these workings to be spoken by you. You must speak the name(s) for Divinity that is within you. This is about your relationship with God-the Great Spirit-the Goddess. This is your relationship to define.

You reap what you sow.

Magick itself is neither good or bad; dark or light. It is the intent in which magick is used that defines the nature of it. The darkest of magick comes from a place of hate, envy, jealously, greed, malice and sloth. We must always strive to come from a place of love and Light in our physical and spiritual worlds.

Remember, as above so below, as within so without. Our lives need to be lived well and honestly, for the blessings of Divinity to surround us. We need to strive to always be in a state of giving, to receive all the blessings, we truly deserve.

In order to ask for God's vengeance, you must be able to stand "righteously before the Lord." This is part of the rules for using the words of destruction and smite in the Psalms. Only those standing in true innocence can judge and be judged without the working turning against them. And remember, you can't fool God.

Myrtle Beach Lady and Crazy Sock were sitting on stools at the counter this Thursday afternoon. Each had a small cup with a shot of rum in it. I was in my usual spot behind the counter, sitting on another stool with a cup of rum in front of me. Thursday is Spirit Day at the shop, which means rum and cigars. Both ladies were being polite, and sipping the rum reserved for the "good" customers.

First question- why is Crazy Sock her shop name? For one very, very, amusing reason. She puts her money in an old, clean athlete sock that she tucks in her bra. The Haitian Priest won't touch her money and one time, washed the bills she gave us.

Now, about Spirit Day. Every Thursday, year-round, the Haitian Priest lights extra candles, says a few more prayers of blessings and gives customers a shot of rum. Good customers get the good rum. Not so good, get the cheap stuff. I smoke cigars in the shop and blow the smoke across various candles, so the Spirits can enjoy too.

I thoroughly appreciate and look forward to both ladies' company. CS is an amazing Florida based conjurer that has embraced both her Caribbean heritage and European side. Like me, we both practice a form of Hoodoo Witchery. It is always nice to have a likeminded person in the shop.

With MB Lady sitting at the counter, we were talking about the mystical uses of numbers. She loves her sacred, magickal numbers. We had just agreed on certain lines of numbers having some ancient, and unknown magick in them, when White Truck made her appearance.

The shift in energy was immediate. MB Lady gave a disapproving snort under her breath, while I poured a shot of the cheap rum for White Truck. Her timing, as always, was right when you really didn't want to see her. She had a knack for showing up when other magickal minded folks were around. Looking for scraps, as always.

The standard "Whatcha doin' Witchery?" was her opening question as she headed toward the counter, quickly spotting the notepad full of numbers.

"Solving the mysteries of the universe. Any suggestions?" I replied dryly.

Both MB Lady and CS sipped their rum and straightened wrinkles in their clothes, that didn't exist. Neither of them held any regard for White Truck. They know exactly what she is all about.

Constantly in a state of receiving, is a nice way of talking about White Truck. Yet, she has very little and always seems to be a couple of weeks away from homelessness. Even if she got a little "somethin-somethin'" going on, it would somehow evaporate or not come to pass. The universe was not working in her favor.

She didn't want to understand the simplicity of what we told her repeatedly. You need to be a good person, for good things to happen. You need to connect to Divinity, and the spirit world if you want to be a powerful Hoodoo practitioner, conjurer, root worker.

Instead, all she wanted was other folks' magick for free, so she could hopefully benefit from it. No real effort, but all the benefits was her goal most of the time. She would get a small moment of success and things would seem to be looking up, then somehow, someway it would go bad. When you asked her about it; always someone else's fault. She never took responsibility for any of her actions.

I handed White Truck the plastic cup with the shot of rum as she sided up to the counter. I wasn't surprised to see her. It was Thursday after all, and you can get a couple shots of free rum at the botanica if you are in the know. Just enough knowledge to take advantage of something on the surface and totally disregard the depth of the day.

"Oooo…them magickal numbers, Witchery?" she inquired while looking closely at the notepad.

"For some folks, yes, very powerful numbers." I replied.

"What do they do?" she wanted to know.

"They be cursin' numbers and you have to know the words to use them." CS's voice gave away her nonsense.

We all laughed, but White Truck pressed on. She knows this is an opportunity with the three of us present, to get some magickal information she could deem useful. We also know, and we are wily Witches.

"It does not matter if I tell you all my magickal numbers, you can't use them, cuz they are mine." MB Lady was the first to weave the web.

"Numbers can't be yours. That makes no sense." White Truck replied. CS and I just shook our heads but didn't say a word.

"Yes, they can. The spirit world done told me." MB Lady smugly replied.

"Well then, how do I get my own magickal numbers?" she demanded.

"Well, it starts with four black chickens." CS says.

"Don't be given White Truck the real advanced magick." I chided CS, "She isn't ready for it."

"Yes, I am. Yes, I am" as she downed her rum and held the cup *up for me to refill.*

"They have to be real black chickens. Not the ones with just a speckle of black feathers." MB lady added. "For real?" White Truck said, wide eyed while the three of us nodded in unison.

"It's THE secret." CS said knowingly.

"We all had to find 4 black, black chickens." I added behind her.

Now just a quick side note; four is typically deemed a neutral or non magickal number. It is perfectly balanced, and we are normally working to tip the scales to our benefit. Most Hoodoo folks don't favor the number four in their workings.

"I don't believe ya'll". White Truck was skeptical and intelligent at her best; a con at her worst. She wanted to hear more.

"You know we sometimes use a chicken or two...."CS started.

"The Haitian Priest does it for clients who want magick." I stated, knowing using his name would carry weight.

"Really? Why are ya'll telling me?" White Truck asked.

"We are friends and it is Spirit Day." MB Lady smiled.

"We have to tell you, cuz we drank rum together. The spirits demand that we tell you how we got our magick. But you can't tell anyone or the magick will go away. That is part of the magick" CS blurted out, then downed the contents of her cup which I quickly refilled.

"Need water blessed by someone who ain't never sinned, to wash your feet with" MB Lady offered up.

"You got to cast a circle of red brick dust from an old church that has burned down on a rainy night" I contributed.

"And all four of them chickens have to stay in the circle while you say the magickal words" CS nodded at her.

With each strand of the web, we gave up questionable directions and ingredients that would be almost, if not downright impossible to acquire. Witchery folk have a reputation for not giving up secrets to sincere seekers so "pieing" someone like White Truck was not a problem. Pieing or pied information is purposeful magickal misinformation given to someone.

At some point, both CS and I drank the full contents of our cups, and I poured another shot of the "good" stuff for both of us. White Truck is started to realize that our super magickal working is anything but magickal.

"All ya'll is bad. Just bad. I know you are foolin' on me. That ain't right. Why you be like that?" she asked, almost annoyed.

"When you get a job maybe you can afford to buy a book with all the answers" MB lady flatly stated.

"You know I have been looking for a job for three years now. Besides I got me a date with a real type businessman. You just never know what is gonna come of it" White Truck shot back while holding up the empty cup for the third time.

"Your electric bill is gonna get paid?" CS said with a sly smile.

We all laughed including White Truck because everyone knew what CS said may very well be true.

I re-filled White Truck's cup with a shot of the "good" rum. She saw the bottle and smiled at me.

Maybe she didn't get any magick today, but at least she got a taste of the top shelf rum.

Poor, poor White Truck, all she must do is look within to find she can change everything.

Properly preparing for successful outcome of workings
Yourself

Always take a good cleansing bath/shower using the best quality soap/bath salts you can find before doing any working.

Suggestions for spiritual bath blends- Rosemary, Ruda or Hyssop blends. There are many well researched magickal herbal books to help you create the perfect blend you need for the start of any working.

Mentally prepare yourself by mediating, listening to music, sitting quietly, whatever is your way. If you don't know your way, try a couple of different things and see which one works the best then, use that method each time. Ultimately you can't yell at the boyfriend, kick the dog and then expect to work positive energies; you need to be in "good head space".

Your energies are the core of any magick you do. Try to build a rhythm or foundation that doesn't really change much each time you do your workings. With familiarity comes the ability to expand and be capable of more. Don't be afraid to experiment. Ultimately, you are developing a highly personalized system of magick that works for you.

What you work in the astral world you must also work in the physical world. Don't just sit there waiting for something to happen. Remember God helps those that help themselves first. If you are looking for employment fill out applications.

Anointing with Oil: Self, a Candle or Other Items

There are many ways to anoint with oil. The goal is to create a sacred item that is going to be used in your working. Many simply say a personal heart felt prayer while holding the item then applying the oil. For anointing yourself the most common way is to anoint forehead, wrists, back of knees and bottom of feet while saying a personal prayer or favorite Psalm.

The Space

Pick a place where you can work without distractions or interruptions. Give yourself plenty of time so you are never rushing your working. Be prepared to put your candle in a place where it can stay undisturbed for the entire time required in the working.

Cleanse the space by using incense, sea salts or herbs to get rid of negative or dark energies. Use a way that relates to you. Which one do you like? Pick and use. Everyone has their own way, develop yours.

The burning of sweet grasses, the passing of a whole, raw egg, and smudging with sage seem to be the most common ways to rid an area of any negative influences. The use of pure unrefined sea salt or old red brick dust are also popular in workings. Both can create a barrier when used by magickal folks.

The Importance of Using Quality Ingredients

Divinity exists in nature. God did not make the universe in a lab and neither should any of your materials be. Pure essential oils; plain, good candles; and real, herbal incense are what were originally used with these prayers and incantations. Always strive to use the very best you can afford.

How long?

Keep a positive outlook from start to finish and be patient. Most of the time you will see results in as early as three days but sometimes the universe needs just a little more time. Look for signs on the 7th day after saying your prayer and again on the 21st day.

If you are working on a major life changing event, don't expect that to happen in a few weeks. Sometimes things take months or years for the universe to line up the way you want. If something is really worth having, then you must have patience and remember the goal.

To Know-To Will-To Dare-To Keep Silent

Take the time to prepare properly. Make sure you completely understand what you are doing. Have no doubts; speak only of "when it happens" never "if it happens." Be very careful speaking of what you have done, it could impact the outcome of your workings. For the best possible outcome-ssshhhhh.....silence

Part 3 We All Do

Embracing that which is already within

I read this on a reply in an online thread to mixing pantheons in personal belief systems. This young man has an old soul that is wiser than our current modern age. He perfectly summed up what Hoodoo/life is all about.

Life is cultural appropriation for those who hunger and pursue truth in all its forms. Once, we were one people, one tradition and in time we will be again. Magick (faith) is (faith) magick, no matter where it's from or form it takes; in studying different cultures and truths I have found more unity in core of beliefs, spiritual systems, creation stories and magick. Define your path by knowledge, wisdom and love and the universe will meet you with all the best lessons.

Prophet Bazahas, Long Island, New York, Eclectic Spiritualist

Pagan, Christian, Spiritualist, Old Religion, New Religion, we can all use Hoodoo. It is a magickal system that can be utilized by anyone.

Hoodoo Toolbox for the Psalms

Items used in the workings for the Psalms are readily available and easy to find. Supplies needed are listed with each working. Check around locally, and support shops in your community. Remember if you buy dollar store supplies you will get dollar store magick. Buying the very best you can afford is part of the offering for the magick you are about to do. What you put in is what you get out.

Incense comes in many different forms. The most popular are stick, cone and loose grains. When using the stick kind, use 3-6 sticks at the same time. For cones, use two at a time and for the loose kind use your preference. Make sure it is made with real essential oils and/or herbs. Have a burner or safe area to light and let it burn for a period of time. If indoors, don't forget to open a window while burning incense.

Essential oil recipes come to us from antiquity. It is very important to use only top quality all-natural oils in any working you do. Some workings call for a certain oil blend, like blessing oil. Either make your own or buy ready-made at most magickal type shops. There are several magickal companies making great ready-to-use blends. Either way just make sure you know what you are getting.

Herbs used should be fresh, organic and/or dried properly without the use of any chemicals. The very best herbs are the ones you can grow yourself. This insures you know the energy that went into your working from start to finish. White sage is very easy to grow and dry. Start with a large pot on the doorstep and see what you can do.

Candles should be solid in color, unscented, and good quality. Types used are taper (approx. 8" tall is a good size) and 7 day glass container. Never blow out a candle. This is very important, let me repeat; never blow out a candle. Pinch it out or let it burn completely out. To blow out a candle is to blow your work away.

Paper to be used is parchment paper, this is a natural unrefined paper. White paper or notebook paper contains chemicals that will effect/affect the outcome of workings. What is normally used in the workings is a quarter of a sheet of standard size parchment paper; fold paper in half and then half again, cut along lines. If a larger size is used it will be noted.

Quick List for Success

1. Assemble all items needed
2. Prepare self
3. Prepare space
4. Do your working

5. Secure space (so it is safe to leave candles unattended if needed)
6. Shhhhh......Silence.

Part 4 Workings

Hoodoo folks work in the spiritual realms with Divinity and Ancestors. They use the energies of the land to help build this magickal connection. They also know that there are tools to help us access and use this power.

The Books of Psalms is one of those tools. It is a very powerful tool that can bring change into your life, and those around you. Blessings and prosperity, wisdom and understanding are all attainable goals within the Psalms. For over 2,000 years the verses of the Psalms have been used to make all these things happen.

Magickal Tidbit
During the time of the New Moon open windows in your house to clear out the old energies and welcome the new ones.
During the time of the Full Moon close all windows before midnight to keep out dark /evil energies.

1

Being Thankful-Blessings-Speaking

In everything give thanks: for this is the will of God in Christ Jesus concerning you. 1 Thessalonians 5:18

O give thanks unto the LORD, for he is good: for his mercy endureth forever. Psalms 107:1

Magickal Tidbit
Plant Rosemary near your doorway to attract friends.
Sprinkle food with Parsley, Sage & Thyme to keep harmony in relationships.

~~~~~~~~~~ *** ~~~~~~~~~~

Psalm 20 - Receiving blessings
Do you have something you desire above all else? This working will grant your wish so long as you are acting in the Light of Divinity. (Not a good working for financial matters; consider using Attracting Wealth - Psalm 68).

Day: All except Wednesday
Incense: Frankincense & Myrrh
Oil: Blessing
Candle: 7 Day-White
Other: Parchment paper, rosemary blend bath salts

Prepare yourself by taking a good cleansing bath with Rosemary blend bath salts. Light the candle and put where it can burn until completely out. While you are saying the verses do the following:

verse 3- light incense, verse 5- write down desire on a piece of parchment, verse 6- anoint forehead with oil. Light parchment paper with candle and burn completely to ash. So mote it be.

Psalm 20 v 1-9

1   *The LORD hear thee in the day of trouble; the name of the God of Jacob defend thee;*

2   *Send thee help from the sanctuary, and strengthen thee out of Zion;*

3   *Remember all thy offerings, and accept thy burnt sacrifice; Selah.*

4   *Grant thee according to thine own heart, and fulfil all thy counsel.*

5   *We will rejoice in thy salvation, and in the name of our God we will set up our banners: the LORD fulfil all thy petitions.*

6   *Now know I that the LORD saveth his anointed; he will hear him from his holy heaven with the saving strength of his right hand.*

7   *Some trust in chariots, and some in horses: but we will remember the name of the LORD our God.*

8   *They are brought down and fallen: but we are risen, and stand upright.*

9   *Save us, LORD: let the king hear us when we call.*

~~~~~~~~~~ *** ~~~~~~~~~~

Psalm 28 - Asking for prayers to be answered

Sometimes a prayer needs a little extra help to hurry it along. Use this working when you are in dire need.

Day: All
Incense: John the Conqueror
Oil: Blessings
Candle: 7 Day- Spiritual White

Other: Seal of Knowledge, Holy water

This is a seven day working best started at sunrise. Burn incense. Put several drops of blessing oil along inside edge of candle while repeating verse. Say aloud the prayer you want to be answered. Place a drop of oil on your forehead and again say verse. Rinse your hands with Holy water and repeat verse again. Each morning while candle burns say verse. Place the Seal of Knowledge in your pillowcase. Leave there until your prayer is answered. So mote it be.

Psalm 28 v 2
Hear the voice of my supplications, when I cry unto thee, when I lift up my hands toward thy holy oracle.

~~~~~~~~~~ *** ~~~~~~~~~~

Psalm 47 - Giving thanks for a blessing
Saying thank you when prayers are answered will help to insure that the blessings continue. This should be done every time you do any workings and have success. Let Divinity know that you are indeed grateful.

Day: All
Incense: 3 Kings
Candle: 7 Day–White

Burn incense and light the candle. Sit quietly mediating on what you are thankful for then read the Psalm. Let candle burn completely out (approx. seven days). Each morning while the candle is burning read the Psalm. So mote it be.

Psalm 47
1   *O clap your hands, all ye people; shout unto God with the voice*

of triumph.

2   For the LORD most high is terrible; he is a great King over all the earth.

3   He shall subdue the people under us, and the nations under our feet. 4 He shall choose our inheritance for us, the excellency of Jacob whom he loved. Selah.

5   God is gone up with a shout, the LORD with the sound of a trumpet.

6   Sing praises to God, sing praises: sing praises unto our King, sing praises.

7   For God is the King of all the earth: sing ye praises with understanding.

8   God reigned over the heathen: God sits upon the throne of his holiness.

9   The princes of the people are gathered together, even the people of the God of Abraham: for the shields of the earth belong unto God: he is greatly exalted.

~~~~~~~~~~ *** ~~~~~~~~~~

Psalm 66 - Giving thanks for answered prayers

When a working gets the desired results or a prayer is answered it is very important to show your gratitude. This will also help to insure that all will go well in your next workings. We should all give twice as many thank yous than we request spiritual aid.

Day: All
Candle: 7 Day-Spirit
Oil: Holy

Anoint candle with oil. Light the candle. Say verses of Psalm aloud. Repeat daily as feel needed. Let candle burn completely out. Do an act of charity or service during this time. So mote it be.

Psalm 66 v 13-16

13 *I will go into thy house with burnt offerings: I will pay thee my vows,*

14 *Which my lips have uttered, and my mouth hath spoken, when I was in trouble.*

15 *I will offer unto thee burnt sacrifices of fatlings, with the incense of rams; I will offer bullocks with goats. Selah.*

16 *Come and hear, all ye that fear God, and I will declare what he hath done for my soul.*

~~~~~~~~~~ *** ~~~~~~~~~~

Psalm 92 - Extra special thanks

When you have received an extra special blessing or gift from the spiritual world you should always show your gratitude. This working will let Divinity know that you are indeed thankful.

Day: All
Candle: 7 Day-Spiritual
Oil: Blessings or Divinity

Anoint candle with oil and light. Say aloud the blessings you have received and then the verses of the Psalm. Repeat daily while the candle burns. So mote it be.

Psalm 92 v 1-2, 4-5, 7-8

1 *It is a good thing to give thanks unto the LORD, and to sing praises unto thy name, O most High:*

2 *To show forth thy loving kindness in the morning, and thy faithfulness every night,*

4 *For thou, LORD, hast made me glad through thy work: I will triumph in the works of thy hands.*

5 *O LORD, how great are thy works! And thy thoughts are very deep.*

31

7   When the wicked spring as the grass, and when all the workers
     of iniquity do flourish; it is that they shall be destroyed forever:
8   But thou, LORD, art most high for evermore.

~~~~~~~~~~ *** ~~~~~~~~~~

Psalm 144 - Being thankful for received blessings

This working should be used daily by those who have received
the continued blessings of Divinity.

Day: All
Candle: 7 Day-White/Spiritual

This is a seven day working. Light the candle while saying verses
of Psalm aloud. Every evening near dusk sit quietly and read
verses of Psalm several times until feel satisfied. So mote it be.

Psalm 144 v 1-2-15

1   Blessed be the LORD my strength, which teaches my hands to
     war, and my fingers to fight:
2   My goodness, and my fortress; my high tower, and my deliverer;
     my shield, and he in whom I trust; who subdues my people
     under me.
15   Happy is that people, that is in such a case: yea, happy is that
     people, whose God is the LORD.

~~~~~~~~~~ *** ~~~~~~~~~~

Psalm 145 - Patience in waiting for a blessing

Having patience is one of the hardest things to do sometimes.
This working will help you to take a deep breath, relax, and
know that the blessing is on its way.

Day: All

Slowly read the verses of Psalm taking in their meaning. Read several times until you feel satisfied. Repeat as needed. So mote it be.

Psalm 145 v 16-21

16 *Thou opens thine hand, and satisfies the desire of every living thing.*

17 *The LORD is righteous in all his ways, and holy in all his works.*

18 *The LORD is nigh unto all them that call upon him, to all that call upon him in truth.*

19 *He will fulfil the desire of them that fear him: he also will hear their cry, and will save them.*

20 *The LORD preserves all them that love him: but all the wicked will he destroy.*

21 *My mouth shall speak the praise of the LORD: and let all flesh bless his holy name forever and ever.*

~~~~~~~~~~ *** ~~~~~~~~~~

Psalm 45 – When speaking in public

Are you fearful of speaking in front of a group of people? Sometimes all we need is a little boost of confidence to let the words flow from within us. This working will help you to achieve this.

Day: All
Herbal Bath: Quince Seed-1 teaspoon, Queen of the Meadow-1 teaspoon, Marigold powder-1 teaspoon, Hops-1 teaspoon, Mace-1 teaspoon
Oil: Success
Other: Crystal quartz point

Combine all herbs in a small pot. Bring to a gentle boil for 15 minutes. Remove from heat and let cool off. Put mixture in dark glass container and place in cool dark place for seven days. Strain mixture to remove bits and pieces of herbs. Use ¼ cup of mixture in your bath and when washing your clothes. Wash crystal point with herbal bath mixture then anoint with success oil while repeating verses over and over until feeling a deep sense of calm. Carry or wear crystal when you have to speak publicly. Do not let other people touch the crystal; if so, do the blessing again. So mote it be.

Psalm 45 v 1 & 2

1   *My heart is inditing a good matter: I speak of the things which I have made touching the king: my tongue is the pen of a ready writer.*

2   *Thou art fairer than the children of men: grace is poured into thy lips: therefore God hath blessed thee forever.*

~~~~~~~~~~ *** ~~~~~~~~~~

Psalm 119 – When you have to ask/speak to Your Boss

Do get nervous or tongue-tied when trying to talk to your boss? Need to ask for a raise? Use this working to get the confidence you need and to say the right words.

Day: All
Herb: Black Snake Root-1 piece
Oil: Success

While reading verses of Psalm aloud anoint root with oil. Keep root with you when talking to your boss. So mote it be.

Psalm 119 v 114-116

114 *Thou art my hiding place and my shield: I hope in thy word.*
115 *Depart from me, ye evildoers: for I will keep the commandments*

of my God.

116 *Uphold me according unto thy word, that I may live: and let me not be ashamed of my hope.*

~~~~~~~~~~ ***** ~~~~~~~~~~

Psalm 122 – When having to speaking to someone important

Use this working to make sure that what you want to say gets heard. Will help to give your words confidence and power. Very good to use when having to speak to bank or financial people to make things go positive for you.

Day: All
Herb: Bay Berry, Senna leaves, Comfrey Bark, Blue Vervain-1 tablespoon each
Oil: Commanding
Other: small red cotton/flannel bag

While saying the verses aloud thirteen times place herbs and couple drops of oil in bag. Tie securely shut. Keep bag in pocket or purse when talking to important person. So mote it be.

Psalm 122 v6-7-8

6   *Pray for the peace of Jerusalem: they shall prosper that love thee.*

7   *Peace be within thy walls, and prosperity within thy palaces.*

8   *For my brethren and companions' sakes, I will now say, Peace be within thee.*

~~~~~~~~~~ ***** ~~~~~~~~~~

Psalm 141 - Thinking before you speak/saying kind words

Words have the ability to lift someone up or tear them down. This working will help you to use your words wisely and kindly.

Day: All
Herbal Incense: Sage (needs to be fresh dried loose leaves)
Herbal Tea: Licorice Root

This is a three day working that needs to be done right after sunset. Each day burn a handful of sage. Sit and read verses over and over until feel a calm come over you. Afterwards drink tea while envisioning yourself as a wise person. So mote it be.

Psalm 141 v 1-2-3

1 *LORD, I cry unto thee: make haste unto me; give ear unto my voice, when I cry unto thee.*

2 *Let my prayer be set forth before thee as incense; and the lifting up of my hands as the evening sacrifice.*

3 *Set a watch, O LORD, before my mouth; keep the door of my lip.*

~~~~~~~~~~ ******* ~~~~~~~~~~

Psalm 149 - Needing courage to speak up

There are times when we must speak of what we know or have seen. Good to use when having to testify against someone. Will help to keep your words true and without malice.

Day: All
Herbal Tea: Peppermint
Oil: Peppermint
Other: Lodestone-1 piece

Dab a small amount of oil on your pillowcase. Sit quietly and read verses of Psalm while holding Lodestone. Keep the stone with you when needed. Let no one touch it. So mote it be.

Psalm 149 v 1-4

1   *Praise ye the LORD. Sing unto the LORD a new song, and his praise in the congregation of saints.*

2   *Let Israel rejoice in him that made him: let the children of Zion be joyful in their King.*

3   *Let them praise his name in the dance: let them sing praises unto him with the timbrel and harp.*

4   *For the LORD taketh pleasure in his people: he will beautify the meek with salvation.*

2

Love-Friends-Home

Do to others as you would have them do to you. Luke 6:31

By wisdom a house is built, and by understanding it is established; by knowledge the rooms are filled with all precious and pleasant riches.
Proverbs 24:3-4

Magickal Tidbit
Never put a burnt match back in the box. This could cause your luck to leave.
A mirror in your entry way will repel negativity.

~~~~~~~~~~ *** ~~~~~~~~~~

Psalm 57 - Healing a broken heart/letting go
Saying good-bye is one of the hardest things to do sometimes. This working will help to ease the pain and open you up for new possibilities.

Day: All
Incense: Orris Root powder-2 teaspoons, Lavender incense-2 teaspoons, Vanilla powder-2 teaspoons, Bayberry powder-2 teaspoons, Dragon's Blood resin-2 teaspoons, Saltpeter-1 teaspoon, Sandalwood powder-2 teaspoons
Candle: Taper-Black
Other: Parchment, Dragon's Blood ink

Blend all incense together and store in air tight container. Write your full name on both sides of parchment paper and place under candle. Light the candle and burn incense. Sit quietly for a time opening yourself up to the peace of God. When feel ready say verses of Psalm aloud. Pinch out candle when done. Repeat daily for nine days. So mote it be.

Psalm 57 v 1-3

1   Be merciful unto me, O God, be merciful unto me: for my soul trusteth in thee: yea, in the shadow of thy wings will I make my refuge, until these calamities be overpast.

2   I will cry unto God most high; unto God that performeth all things for me.

3   He shall send from heaven, and save me from the reproach of him that would swallow me up. Selah. God shall send forth his mercy and his truth.

~~~~~~~~~~ *** ~~~~~~~~~~

Psalm 111 - Finding true love

Are you ready to find your true love soul-mate? From hoodoo antiquity this is a wonderful working that has claimed many successes. Based on notes found in an early colonial attic in Charleston, South Carolina that appears to have even earlier roots.

Day: New Moon
Herbal Bath: Orris powder-1 teaspoons, Lemongrass-3 teaspoons, Lavender-4 teaspoons, Rosemary-4 teaspoons

Blend ingredients and let seep in gallon of spring water for two days. While blending say verses of Psalms aloud. Use ¼ cup of mixture in your bath until meet your future mate. Herbal mixture is good for about two weeks. So mote it be.

Psalm 111 v 1-2-3-7-8-9

1   Praise ye the LORD. I will praise the LORD with my whole

heart, in the assembly of the upright, and in the congregation.

2   *The works of the LORD are great, sought out of all them that have pleasure therein.*

3   *His work is honourable and glorious: and his righteousness endureth forever.*

7   *The works of his hands are verity and judgment; all his commandments are sure.*

8   *They stand fast for ever and ever, and are done in truth and uprightness.*

9   *He sent redemption unto his people: he hath commanded his covenant forever: holy and reverend is his name.*

~~~~~~~~~~ *** ~~~~~~~~~~

Psalm 111 - Attracting friends

When seeking new friends you want to attract positive, successful people who have God in their lives. Use this working to help aid you achieve this.

Day: All
Herb: Mugwort, Lavender, Blue Vervain
Candle: 7 Day-White Spiritual

Use incense, bath soap or oils, teas, etcetera that contain the listed herbs. Burn candle, incense and read verses of Psalm daily. So mote it be.

Psalm 111 v 1-5

1   *Praise ye the LORD. I will praise the LORD with my whole heart, in the assembly of the upright, and in the congregation.*

2   *The works of the LORD are great, sought out of all them that have pleasure therein.*

3   *His work is honorable and glorious: and his righteousness endureth forever.*

4   *He hath made his wonderful works to be remembered: the LORD is gracious and full of compassion.*

5   *He hath given meat unto them that fear him: he will ever be mindful of his covenant.*

~~~~~~~~~~ *** ~~~~~~~~~~

Psalm 123 - Seeking to keep your friends close

This is a very good working to use for drawing your friends closer to you. Very helpful in keeping your friends loyal and on your side.

Day: All
Incense: Lotus
Herb-Blue: Vervain-2 tablespoons, Irish Moss-3 small pieces
Oil: Attraction

Burn incense and anoint self with oil daily for seven days in the morning. Sprinkle small amount of Blue Vervain across your front doorstep each day. Place pieces of Irish moss under your bed and leave them there. Read verses of Psalm daily during seven days. So mote it be.

Psalm 123

1   *Unto thee lift I up mine eyes, O thou that dwellest in the heavens.*

2   *Behold, as the eyes of servants look unto the hand of their masters, and as the eyes of a maiden unto the hand of her mistress; so our eyes wait upon the LORD our God, until that he have mercy upon us.*

3   *Have mercy upon us, O LORD, have mercy upon us: for we are exceedingly filled with contempt.*

4   *Our soul is exceedingly filled with the scorning of those that are at ease, and with the contempt of the proud.*

~~~~~~~~~~ *** ~~~~~~~~~~

Psalm 61 - Looking for a new home

Wanting to find a safe and secure neighborhood to live in? Use this working to help achieve that goal. Let the Spirits of Divinity aid and guide you in finding the right place.

Day: All
Candle: -7 Power
Other: Dove's Blood ink, parchment paper

Write your full name using Dove's Blood ink on the parchment paper three times. On other side of paper draw a simple house with three circles around it. On top of house write the verses of the Psalm below. Place paper under candle and light the candle. Let candle burn completely out. Fold paper and keep in your wallet until you find the home you desire. So mote it be.

Psalm 61 v 1-3

1   Hear my cry, O God; attend unto my prayer.
2   From the end of the earth will I cry unto thee, when my heart is overwhelmed: lead me to the rock that is higher than I.
3   For thou hast been a shelter for me, and a strong tower from the enemy.

~~~~~~~~~~ *** ~~~~~~~~~~

Psalm 84 - Blessing a new home

It is very important to clear out old and negative energies from your new home. If left to linger, the energies could influence, harm, cause bad luck or lack of wealth.

Day: New Moon
Incense: Wood Betony-2 teaspoon, Vanillan-2 teaspoon, Sage-

1/2 cup
Candle: 7 day White Spiritual
Oil: Holy
Other: Holy Water

Combine incense ingredients together and store in air tight container. On the first morning of the new moon place candle as close to center in your home as you can. Next burn small dish of incense in every room. Light the candle and say verses aloud three times. When the last rays of the sun go down burn more incense in each room and again say verses aloud three times. Let candle burn completely out. So mote it be.

Psalm 84 v 1-4

1   *How amiable are thy tabernacles, O LORD of hosts!*

2   *My soul longeth, yea, even fainteth for the courts of the LORD: my heart and my flesh crieth out for the living God.*

3   *Yea, the sparrow hath found an house, and the swallow a nest for herself, where she may lay her young, even thine altars, O LORD of hosts, my King, and my God.*

4   *Blessed are they that dwell in thy house: they will be still praising thee. Selah.*

~~~~~~~~~~ ***** ~~~~~~~~~~

Psalm 108 - Blessing a newly built home
Use this working for a newly built residence. Fill your new space with the love and light of Divinity, don't let evil and negativity have any opportunity to influence your family's happiness and prosperity.

Day: All
Candle: 7 Day-White Spirit/Divinity
Incense: Sage

Other: Sea salt

Burn sage in all rooms of house, sprinkle small amount of sea salt in all corners. Light the candle and say verses of Psalm aloud daily for as long as candle burns. So mote it be.

Psalm 108

1   *O God, my heart is fixed; I will sing and give praise, even with my glory.*

2   *Awake, psaltery and harp: I myself will awake early.*

3   *I will praise thee, O LORD, among the people: and I will sing praises unto thee among the nations.*

4   *For thy mercy is great above the heavens: and thy truth reacheth unto the clouds.*

5   *Be thou exalted, O God, above the heavens: and thy glory above all the earth;*

6   *That thy beloved may be delivered: save with thy right hand, and answer me.*

7   *God hath spoken in his holiness; I will rejoice, I will divide Shechem, and mete out the valley of Succoth.*

8   *Gilead is mine; Manasseh is mine; Ephraim also is the strength of mine head; Judah is my lawgiver;*

9   *Moab is my washpot; over Edom will I cast out my shoe; over Philistia will I triumph.*

10 *Who will bring me into the strong city? Who will lead me into Edom?*

11 *Wilt not thou, O God, who hast cast us off? And wilt not thou, O God, go forth with our hosts?*

12 *Give us help from trouble: for vain is the help of man.*

13 *Through God we shall do valiantly: for he it is that shall tread down our enemies.*

~~~~~~~~~~ *** ~~~~~~~~~~

Psalm 91 - Safety at home

To make your home a safe place to live and be prosperous use this working. Also said to help stop accidents in your home.

Day: All
Other: Parchment paper, Dragon's blood ink

Using either your own blood or Dragon's blood ink draw large cross on parchment paper and write down all people's names living in the house around the cross. On other side of parchment paper write the verses of the Psalm. Fold paper three times and bury beside front door/step. So mote it be.

Psalm 91 v 9-10, 14-16

9   Because I hast made the LORD, which is my refuge, even the most High, my habitation;

10   There shall no evil befall me, neither shall any plague come nigh my dwelling.

14   Because he hath set his love upon me, therefore will I deliver him: I will set him on high, because he hath known my name.

15   He shall call upon me, and I will answer him: I will be with him in trouble; I will deliver him, and honour him.

16   With long life will I satisfy him, and show him my salvation.

~~~~~~~~~~ *** ~~~~~~~~~~

Psalm 96 - Cleansing a house of negativity

When you feel that dark energies might be lurking in dark corners of your house use this working to rid of any negative influences there may be. And don't forget the attic or basement if you have one.

Day: All
Candle: 7 Day-White Spiritual

Incense: Wood Betony-3 teaspoons, Frankincense-1/2 cup, Orris Root powder-2 teaspoons, Saltpeter-1\2 teaspoon, Sandalwood powder 1 ½ cups
Other: two oranges, 2 apples, 3 limes, cigar, pieces of candy, glass of water

This is a seven day working. Mix incense mixture together and store in an air tight container. Light the candle and place oranges, limes, cigar, candy and glass of water around the candle. You should make the offering look presentable. Each morning burn a little incense mixture in all rooms of the house and read the verses of the Psalm. So mote it be.

Psalm 96 v 6- 9

6   *Honour and majesty are before him: strength and beauty are in his sanctuary.*

7   *Give unto the LORD, O ye kindreds of the people, give unto the LORD glory and strength.*

8   *Give unto the LORD the glory due unto his name: bring an offering, and come into his courts.*

9   *O worship the LORD in the beauty of holiness: fear before him, all the earth.*

~~~~~~~~~~ *** ~~~~~~~~~~

Psalm 128 - Happy/Healthy home blessings/ newlyweds

This working is a wonderful arts and crafts creation. Make a wreath full of herbal energies to fill your home and life with blessings. Best when given as a gift to newlyweds.

Day: All
Dried Herbs/Flowers: Statice, Lavender, Rosemary, Sage, Thyme, 13 small dried red rose buds

Oil: Blessings and/or Divine Savior
Other: Wreath form-10" is good size (can be larger just need more herbs to fill in space), parchment paper, Dragon's blood ink, red and white ribbons twisted together

Anoint wreath form with oil/s. Using flowers, herbs and ribbons fill in wreath form. A hot glue gun works well for this. Write all verses of the Psalm on parchment paper using Dragon's blood ink. Fold parchment paper and secure to back of wreath. Hang wreath over the bed of the couple. So mote it be.

Psalm 128

1   *Blessed is every one that feareth the LORD; that walketh in his ways.*

2   *For thou shalt eat the labour of thine hands: happy shalt thou be, and it shall be well with thee.*

3   *Thy wife shall be as a fruitful vine by the sides of thine house: thy children like olive plants round about thy table.*

4   *Behold, that thus shall the man be blessed that feareth the LORD.*

5   *The LORD shall bless thee out of Zion: and thou shalt see the good of Jerusalem all the days of thy life.*

6   *Yea, thou shalt see thy children's children, and peace upon Israel.*

~~~~~~~~~~ *** ~~~~~~~~~~

Psalm 132 - Seeking a permanent place to live

This Psalm is one of the Songs of David. Use this working for when you have found the place that you know is where you want to be forever. It will help to insure that it will always be yours.

Day: All
Incense: House Blessing powder-1/2 cup, Sandalwood-1/2 cup,

Red clover (crushed)-2 teaspoons, Orris powder-2 teaspoons
Oil: House Blessing
Candle: Taper-Purple
Other: Holy Water, sea salt

Blend all incense ingredients together and store in an air tight container. Anoint candle with water and oil. Place it close to center of house. In each room of the house burn small amount of incense in a fire safe dish. While saying verses aloud sprinkle water and salt across all outside doorways of home and in corners of all rooms. Let candle burn completely out. So mote it be.

Psalm 132 v 15-16-17-18

15 *I will abundantly bless her provision: I will satisfy her poor with bread.*

16 *I will also clothe her priests with salvation: and her saints shall shout aloud for joy.*

17 *There will I make the horn of David to bud: I have ordained a lamp for mine anointed.*

18 *His enemies will I clothe with shame: but upon himself shall his crown flourish.*

3

Health-Comfort-Divine Healing

*You who have made me see many troubles and calamities will revive
me again; from the depths of the earth you will bring me up again. You
will increase my greatness and comfort me again. Psalms 71:20-21*

*My child, be attentive to my words; incline your ear to my sayings.
Do not let them escape from your sight; keep them within your heart.
For they are life to those who find them, and healing to all their flesh.
Proverbs 4:20-22*

Magickal Tidbit
Use the Farmer's Almanac for your magickal calendar.

~~~~~~~~~~ *** ~~~~~~~~~~

Psalm 4 - Restful sleep - stopping nightmares
Trouble sleeping? Having nightmares or evil influences in your
dreams? Here is a wonderful way to get a good night's sleep.
Let the Angels of the Lord wrap their loving arms around you in
your slumber and keep you safe.

Day: All
Herb: Lavender oil
Other: Parchment paper, small red wool bag, red thread/yarn/
string, dragon's blood ink

Write verse three times on parchment paper using dragon's blood
ink (use both sides if needed). Dab Lavender oil on all corners of
paper then fold paper in half three times. Place in the bag and wrap
opening shut with red thread wrapping nine times. Place bag in

corner of pillow case or under mattress at top of bed. So mote it be.

Psalm 4 v.8

I will both lay me down in peace, and sleep: for thou, LORD, only makes me dwell in safety.

~~~~~~~~~~ *** ~~~~~~~~~~

Psalm 56 - Overcoming illness/regaining good health

The power of Divinity is endless and miracles happen daily. Absolute faith and belief will conquer all.

Day: All
Candle: White 7 day Divinity
Oil: Health Healing
Herbal: Bath-Holy Herbs (can purchase already blended or make your own blend with the following ingredients- equal amounts of: Mugwort powder, Hops powder, Jasmine powder, Skullcap powder, Black Cohosh powder, Catnip powder, Peppermint powder).

Seep Holy Herbs in a gallon of hot water for at least 1 hour before using. Anoint candle with oil and light. Read verses of Psalms aloud. Take a long hot bath using ¼ cup of Holy Herbs seeped water in your bath water. Place a dab of Healthy Healing oil on your forehead after bath. Repeat bath daily for seven days or as long as the candle burns. So mote it be.

Psalm 56 v 10-13

10 *In God will I praise his word: in the LORD will I praise his word.*

11 *In God have I put my trust: I will not be afraid what man can do unto me.*

12 *Thy vows are upon me, O God: I will render praises unto thee.*

13   *For thou hast delivered my soul from death: wilt not thou
deliver my feet from falling, that I may walk before God in the
light of the living?*

~~~~~~~~~~ *** ~~~~~~~~~~

Psalm 69 - Lifting/Stopping depression

Let the Joy of Divinity lift you up from your darkness and
surround you in the Light of Goodness and Hope. Use this herbal
bath working to help cleanse and raise your spirit.

Day: All
Incense: Uncrossing
Oil: Peace
Herbal Bath: Blue Vervain-2 tablespoons, Lavender-2
tablespoons, Broom Herb-1 teaspoon
Other: Spring water

Blend herbs and let seep for three days in a quart of spring water
in a cool dark place. Afterwards take mixture and strain out bits
and pieces. Add 10 drops each of Peace and Uncrossing oils to
mixture. Draw yourself a warm bath and add approximately ¼
cup of mixture (shake well before using) to water. Burn incense
in the bathroom. Take a nice leisurely bath. Afterwards read the
verses of the Psalm before going to bed each night for seven days.
Use bath mixture whenever you feel the need. Mixture should be
stored in an airtight container in a cool dark place. Remember to
shake well before using each time. It can be used for up to 30 days
then needs to be thrown out. So mote it be.

Psalm 69 v 13-16

13   *But as for me, my prayer is unto thee, O Lord, in an acceptable
time: O God, in the multitude of thy mercy hear me, in the
truth of thy salvation.*

14 Deliver me out of the mire, and let me not sink: let me be
    delivered from them that hate me, and out of the deep waters.
15 Let not the waterflood overflow me, neither let the deep swallow
    me up, and let not the pit shut her mouth upon me.
16 Hear me, O Lord; for thy loving kindness is good: turn unto me
    according to the multitude of thy tender mercies.

~~~~~~~~~~ *** ~~~~~~~~~~

Psalm 89 - Healing a sickness

This working is a very powerful combination of a Psalm used
from the time of the early Hebrews to heal sickness and the use
of ancient magickal words for healing.

Day: All
Oil: Healing
Candle: 7 Day-White/Spiritual
Other: Parchment paper-full sheet, dove's blood ink

On one side of parchment paper write person to be healed full
birth name using dove's blood ink. Draw three circles around
the name with each circle bigger. On the other side of the paper,
using dove's blood ink, write down the following exactly:

ABRACADABRA
ABRACADABR
ABRACADAB
ABRACADA
ABRACAD
ABRACA
ABRAC
ABRA
ABR
AB
A

Anoint yourself, candle and paper with healing oil. Fold paper in half and place under white spiritual candle. Light the candle and say verses of Psalm aloud several times until feel satisfied. Let candle completely burn out (approx. seven days). Repeat if feel needed. So mote it be.

Psalm 89 v 1-5, 15-18

1   *I will sing of the mercies of the LORD forever: with my mouth will I make known thy faithfulness to all generations.*

2   *For I have said, Mercy shall be built up forever: thy faithfulness shalt thou establish in the very heavens.*

3   *I have made a covenant with my chosen, I have sworn unto David my servant,*

4   *Thy seed will I establish forever, and build up thy throne to all generations. Selah.*

5   *And the heavens shall praise thy wonders, O LORD: thy faithfulness also in the congregation of the saints.*

15   *Blessed is the people that know the joyful sound: they shall walk, O LORD, in the light of thy countenance.*

16   *In thy name shall they rejoice all the day: and in thy righteousness shall they be exalted.*

17   *For thou art the glory of their strength: and in thy favour our horn shall be exalted.*

18   *For the LORD is our defense; and the Holy One of Israel is our king.*

~~~~~~~~~~ *** ~~~~~~~~~~

Psalm 105 - Easing a headache

This working is based upon a tried and true formula that has been said to be very successful. Rosemary and Lavender can always be found in any well stocked magickal cabinet.

Day: All
Herb: Rosemary or/and Lavender infused tea, fresh Lavender
and Rosemary
Oil: Lavender

You can find Rosemary/Lavender teas at most healthy food stores.
It is very easy to infuse any tea of your choice with Rosemary/
Lavender by simply seeping fresh herbs for a couple of minutes
in the tea. It is also recommended to use fresh Rosemary in all
your meals. Dab Lavender on your temples and pulse points on
wrists when you feel a headache coming. Sit quietly and read
verses of Psalm several times aloud. So mote it be.

Psalm 105 v 39-41

39 *He spread a cloud for a covering; and fire to give light in the
    night.*
40 *The people asked, and he brought quails, and satisfied them
    with the bread of heaven.*
41 *He opened the rock, and the waters gushed out; they ran in the
    dry places like a river.*

~~~~~~~~~~ *** ~~~~~~~~~~

Psalm 119 - Easing a headache

The combination of spiritual and herbal ingredients make this a
very effective working.

Day: All
Incense: Lavender
Herbal Tea: Willow bark infusion
Oil: Peace, Lavender

Burn incense and place a dab of peace oil on your forehead. Put
lavender oil on your temples and the inside of your wrists. Sit

quietly, drink tea and read verses of the Psalm aloud several times. Repeat as needed. So mote it be.

Psalm 119 v 165-168

165 *Great peace have they which love thy law: and nothing shall offend them. 166 LORD, I have hoped for thy salvation, and done thy commandments.*

167 *My soul hath kept thy testimonies; and I love them exceedingly.*

168 *I have kept thy precepts and thy testimonies: for all my ways are before thee.*

~~~~~~~~~~ *** ~~~~~~~~~~

Psalm 119 - Taking away pain in the liver, kidney or hips

There is medical evidence that lemons and dandelion root will help with issues in the kidneys. Always consult your doctor and do research before starting any herbal remedies.

Day: All

Herbal Tea: Dandelion Root-2 teaspoons or 1 bag

Other: Fresh Lemon juice-2 tablespoons, honey to taste

Seep Dandelion Root in cup of hot water for several minutes. Remove herb/bag and add lemon juice. Lemon juice should be fresh squeezed. While drinking tea read verses of Psalm several times. So mote it be.

Psalm 119 v65-68 & 71-72

65 *Thou hast dealt well with thy servant, O LORD, according unto thy word.*

66 *Teach me good judgment and knowledge: for I have believed thy commandments.*

67 *Before I was afflicted I went astray: but now have I kept thy*

word.

68 *Thou art good, and doest good; teach me thy statutes.*

71 *It is good for me that I have been afflicted; that I might learn thy statutes.*

72 *The law of thy mouth is better unto me than thousands of gold and silver.*

~~~~~~~~~~ *** ~~~~~~~~~~

Psalm 119 - Relieving body pain

This recipe for an herbal bath is very good for all over weariness and muscle aches. Use whenever needed.

Day: All
Incense: Aloe Vera
Herbal Bath: Spearmint leaves (dried, crushed)-2 tablespoons, Willow bark (crushed)-2 tablespoons, Dill Weed-2 teaspoons, Lavender-2 tablespoons
Oil: Eucalyptus-7 drops

Burn incense in bathroom before bathing. Combine herbs and seep in gallon of spring water for three days. Strain and use ½ cup of water in your bath. Add Eucalyptus oil to bath water while water is running. Afterwards sit quietly and read verses of Psalm several times. Do this daily until you feel better. Herbal bath mixture is good for 30 days. So mote it be.

Psalm 119 v 121-128

121 *I have done judgment and justice: leave me not to mine oppressors.*

122 *Be surety for thy servant for good: let not the proud oppress me.*

123 *Mine eyes fail for thy salvation, and for the word of thy righteousness.*

124 *Deal with thy servant according unto thy mercy, and teach me*

thy statutes.

125 *I am thy servant; give me understanding, that I may know thy testimonies.*

126 *It is time for thee, LORD, to work: for they have made void thy law.*

127 *Therefore I love thy commandments above gold; yea, above fine gold.*

128 *Therefore I esteem all thy precepts concerning all things to be right; and I hate every false way.*

~~~~~~~~~~ *** ~~~~~~~~~~

Psalm 119 - Restoring health

When you have faith all things are possible. Once you do this working never speak of 'if it happens' only 'when it happens.' You must be positive in every way.

Day: All
Herbal Incense: Blessing incense-1 tablespoon, Orris Root powder-2 teaspoons, Mystic Rites-1 tablespoon, Cascara Sagrada-1 teaspoon, Saltpeter-1/2 teaspoon, Lavender-2 teaspoons
Oil: Blessings
Candle: 7 Day-Spiritual/White
Other: Parchment paper, Dragon's blood ink

Blend incense ingredients together and burn a small amount of mixture. Anoint candle with oil and light. Write your full birth name on paper nine times using Dragon's blood ink. Fold paper in half and put under candle. Sit quietly in front of candle and say verses of the Psalm aloud several times. Leave candle to burn. Next two mornings upon rising burn a small amount of incense mixture and read the verses of the Psalm. So mote it be.

Psalm 119 153-154-159-160

153 *Consider mine affliction, and deliver me: for I do not forget thy law.*

154 *Plead my cause, and deliver me: quicken me according to thy word.*

159 *Consider how I love thy precepts: quicken me, O LORD, according to thy loving kindness.*

160 *Thy word is true from the beginning: and every one of thy righteous judgments endureth forever.*

~~~~~~~~~~ *** ~~~~~~~~~~

Psalm 146 - Successful surgery/dentist

Use this working to help make sure that everything goes well during and after surgery. Also good if having to go to the dentist.

Day: All
Herb: High John root-1 piece
Oil: Healthy Healing
Other: red flannel/cotton bag

Anoint High John root and self with oil. Place root in bag. While holding bag say verses of Psalm aloud. Keep bag in your left pocket until healed. On day of surgery put dab of oil on the bottoms of your feet. So mote it be.

Psalm 146

1 *Praise ye the LORD. Praise the LORD, O my soul.*

2 *While I live will I praise the LORD: I will sing praises unto my God while I have any being.*

3 *Put not your trust in princes, nor in the son of man, in whom there is no help.*

4 *His breath goeth forth, he returneth to his earth; in that very day his thoughts perish.*

5   *Happy is he that hath the God of Jacob for his help, whose hope is in the LORD his God:*

6   *Which made heaven, and earth, the sea, and all that therein is: which keepeth truth forever:*

7   *Which executeth judgment for the oppressed: which giveth food to the hungry. The LORD looseth the prisoners:*

8   *The LORD openeth the eyes of the blind: the LORD raiseth them that are bowed down: the LORD loveth the righteous:*

9   *The LORD preserveth the strangers; he relieveth the fatherless and widow: but the way of the wicked he turneth upside down.*

10   *The LORD shall reign forever, even thy God, O Zion, unto all generations. Praise ye the LORD.*

~~~~~~~~~~ *** ~~~~~~~~~~

Psalm 147 - Fast healing

Call upon the great power of God to aid you in healing or recovering from wounds or sickness.

Day: All
Candle: 7 Day-Miracle Healing Power
Oil: Divine Healing

Anoint self and candle with oil. Light the candle. Each morning upon rising read verses of Psalm and anoint self with oil for as long as candle burns (approximately 6-seven days). So mote it be.

Psalm 147 v 1-5

1   *Praise ye the LORD: for it is good to sing praises unto our God; for it is pleasant; and praise is comely.*

2   *The LORD doth build up Jerusalem: he gathered together the outcasts of Israel.*

3   *He healed the broken in heart, and binded up their wounds.*

4   *He told the number of the stars; he called them all by their*

names.

5   *Great is our Lord, and of great power: his understanding is*
     infinite.

~~~~~~~~~~ *** ~~~~~~~~~~

Psalm 85 - Finding peace within

God will forgive you, but will you forgive yourself? This working
will help you to let go of the past and move forward in the Light
of God. Will also help to bring calmness to the mind.

Day: All
Incense: Ruda
Other: Ruda Soap

For seven days burn incense in your home, use soap daily and
read verses every night before going to bed. So mote it be.

Psalm 85 v 7-13

7   *Show us thy mercy, O LORD, and grant us thy salvation.*
8   *I will hear what God the LORD will speak: for he will speak*
     peace unto his people, and to his saints: but let them not turn
     again to folly.
9   *Surely his salvation is nigh them that fear him; that glory*
     may dwell in our land. 10 Mercy and truth are met together;
     righteousness and peace have kissed each other.
11   *Truth shall spring out of the earth; and righteousness shall look*
     down from heaven.
12   *Yea, the LORD shall give that which is good; and our land shall*
     yield her increase.
13   *Righteousness shall go before him; and shall set us in the way*
     of his steps.

~~~~~~~~~~ *** ~~~~~~~~~~

Psalm 90 - Seeking comfort/wisdom

This Psalm is a prayer of Moses. He said this to God when seeking comfort and reassurance during times of persecution. When you are feeling overwhelmed and without anyone to turn to this working will bring the peace and comfort of knowing God is always with you.

Day: All

Incense: Nutmeg, Orris Root & Wood Bettany -1 teaspoon each, pinch of saltpeter, Sandalwood: 2 teaspoons

Mix incense blend together and store in airtight container. Mixture is good for 30 days. Burn incense in center of house and sit quietly and read verses of Psalm whenever feel the need. So mote it be.

Psalm 90 v 12 & 17

12 *So teach us to number our days, that we may apply our hearts unto wisdom.*

17 *And let the beauty of the LORD our God be upon us: and establish thou the work of our hands upon us; yea, the work of our hands establish thou it.*

~~~~~~~~~~ ******* ~~~~~~~~~~

Psalm 96 - Seeking comfort/uncertainty

When faced with uncertainty or a major transition in your life (divorce, moving, death) use this working to gather the spiritual strength to move forward in your life's journey.

Day: All
Incense: Uncrossing
Oil: Peace
Other: Dragon's Blood bath crystals

Draw a warm bath, add Dragon's Blood bath crystals and 10 drops peace oil. Burn uncrossing incense close by. When done sit quietly and read verses of Psalm. Repeat as needed. So mote it be.

Psalm 96 v 1-6

1   *O sing unto the LORD a new song: sing unto the LORD, all the earth.*

2   *Sing unto the LORD, bless his name; show forth his salvation from day to day.*

3   *Declare his glory among the heathen, his wonders among all people.*

4   *For the LORD is great, and greatly to be praised: he is to be feared above all gods.*

5   *For all the gods of the nations are idols: but the LORD made the heavens.*

6   *Honour and majesty are before him: strength and beauty are in his sanctuary.*

~~~~~~~~~~ *** ~~~~~~~~~~

Psalm 141 - Seeking peace of mind

Full of worry and stress? Having a hard time turning off your brain? Can't relax? This working will help to quiet the mind and fill you with calm.

Day: All
Incense: John the Conqueror, Helping Hand
Candle: 7 Day-Divinity
Oil: Peace

Anoint self and candle with oil. Light the candle while saying verses of the Psalm. Bun equal amounts of incense. Sit quietly and read verses of Psalm several times. Repeat as feel necessary. So mote it be.

Psalm 141 v 1-5

1   LORD, I cry unto thee: make haste unto me; give ear unto my voice, when I cry unto thee.

2   Let my prayer be set forth before thee as incense; and the lifting up of my hands as the evening sacrifice.

3   Set a watch, O LORD, before my mouth; keep the door of my lips.

4   Incline not my heart to any evil thing, to practice wicked works with men that work iniquity: and let me not eat of their dainties.

5   Let the righteous smite me; it shall be a kindness: and let him reprove me; it shall be an excellent oil, which shall not break my head: for yet my prayer also shall be in their calamities.

~~~~~~~~~~ *** ~~~~~~~~~~

Psalm 143 - Feeling lost and without hope

Use this working to fill you with the Light of Divinity and to receive all the blessings you deserve.

Day: Wednesday
Incense: Uncrossing
Candle: Taper-Purple
Oil: Blessing
Other: Toothpick, parchment paper

Use a toothpick to write your birth name into candle. Anoint candle and self with oil. Burn incense. Light the candle while saying verses of Psalm aloud. Write down the following on parchment paper three times-'I am a child of the Lord. His blessings are mine to receive.' On the other side of paper draw a large cross. Write your full birth name across the cross. Place paper near candle. Let candle burn until almost done then pinch out. Wrap paper around what is left of candle and place under your mattress at foot of bed. So mote it be.

Psalm 143 v 1-4-5-6-7-8-10-11

1   *Hear my prayer, O LORD, give ear to my supplications: in thy faithfulness answer me, and in thy righteousness.*

4   *Therefore is my spirit overwhelmed within me; my heart within me is desolate. 5 I remember the days of old; I meditate on all thy works; I muse on the work of thy hands.*

6   *I stretch forth my hands unto thee: my soul thirsteth after thee, as a thirsty land. Selah.*

7   *Hear me speedily, O LORD: my spirit faileth: hide not thy face from me, lest I be like unto them that go down into the pit.*

8   *Cause me to hear thy loving kindness in the morning; for in thee do I trust: cause me to know the way wherein I should walk; for I lift up my soul unto thee.*

10   *Teach me to do thy will; for thou art my God: thy spirit is good; lead me into the land of uprightness.*

11   *Quicken me, O LORD, for thy name's sake: for thy righteousness' sake bring my soul out of trouble.*

~~~~~~~~~~ *** ~~~~~~~~~~

Psalm 102 - Receiving divine healing

This working is good for physical, mental, and spiritual healings. The magickal word ABRACALAM is said to have developed in ancient times. Its use is still very popular today.

Day: All
Candle: 7 Day-White
Oil: Healing
Other: Parchment paper, Dove's Blood ink

Anoint candle with oil and light. Anoint self with oil and read verses of Psalm aloud. On parchment paper using Dove's Blood ink write down the following exactly:

ABRACALAM
ABRACALA
ABRACAL
ABRACA
ABRAC
ABRA
ABR
AB
A

On the backside of the paper write the full birth name of the person to be healed. Dab corners of paper with oil. Fold paper three times and place under person's mattress at head of bed. Each day as long as candle burns say verses of Psalm aloud. So mote it be.

Psalm 102 v 1-2-3-11-12-13-24

1   *Hear my prayer, O LORD, and let my cry come unto thee.*

2   *Hide not thy face from me in the day when I am in trouble; incline thine ear unto me: in the day when I call answer me speedily.*

3   *For my days are consumed like smoke, and my bones are burned as an hearth.*

11 *My days are like a shadow that declineth; and I am withered like grass.*

12 *But thou, O LORD, shalt endure forever; and thy remembrance unto all generations.*

13 *Thou shalt arise, and have mercy upon Zion: for the time to favour her, yea, the set time, is come.*

24 *I said, O my God, take me not away in the midst of my days: thy years are throughout all generations.*

~~~~~~~~~~ ***** ~~~~~~~~~~

Psalm 127 - Curing a child

Use this Song of Solomon to help aid you when seeking the divine healing of a child. This working requires unwavering faith and belief.

Day: All
Herbal Bath: Hyssop blend
Oil: Healing, Divine Savior
Candles: 7 Day-Divine Savior

This is a 9 day working and will require two candles. As soon as one candle goes out anoint and light the next candle. To start with anoint candle and child with oils. Light the candle and say Psalm aloud. Give child a bath each night using Hyssop blend and three drops of each oil in bathwater. Afterwards hold the child and say Psalm aloud. Do this for a total of nine nights. Let last candle burn completely out. So mote it be.

Psalm 127

1   Except the LORD build the house, they labour in vain that build it: except the LORD keep the city, the watchman waketh but in vain.

2   It is vain for you to rise up early, to sit up late, to eat the bread of sorrows: for so he giveth his beloved sleep.

3   Lo, children are an heritage of the LORD: and the fruit of the womb is his reward.

4   As arrows are in the hand of a mighty man; so are children of the youth.

5   Happy is the man that hath his quiver full of them: they shall not be ashamed, but they shall speak with the enemies in the gate.

~~~~~~~~~~ *** ~~~~~~~~~~

Psalm 90 - Easing the fear of dying

Let God reassure you that the time the spirit leaves the body is a joyous moment and not to be feared.

Day: All

Other: Seal of Spiritual Assistance

Place Seal under mattress at head of bed. Read Psalm whenever feel the need. So mote it be.

Psalm 90

1   *Lord, thou hast been our dwelling place in all generations.*

2   *Before the mountains were brought forth, or ever thou hadst formed the earth and the world, even from everlasting to everlasting, thou art God.*

3   *Thou turnest man to destruction; and sayest, Return, ye children of men.*

4   *For a thousand years in thy sight are but as yesterday when it is past, and as a watch in the night.*

5   *Thou carriest them away as with a flood; they are as a sleep: in the morning they are like grass which groweth up.*

6   *In the morning it flourisheth, and groweth up; in the evening it is cut down, and withereth.*

7   *For we are consumed by thine anger, and by thy wrath are we troubled.*

8   *Thou hast set our iniquities before thee, our secret sins in the light of thy countenance.*

9   *For all our days are passed away in thy wrath: we spend our years as a tale that is told.*

10   *The days of our years are threescore years and ten; and if by reason of strength they be fourscore years, yet is their strength labour and sorrow; for it is soon cut off, and we fly away.*

11   *Who knoweth the power of thine anger? even according to thy fear, so is thy wrath.*

12   *So teach us to number our days, that we may apply our hearts unto wisdom.*

13   *Return, O LORD, how long? and let it repent thee concerning thy servants.*

14   *O satisfy us early with thy mercy; that we may rejoice and be glad all our days. 15 Make us glad according to the days wherein thou hast afflicted us, and the years wherein we have seen evil.*

16   *Let thy work appear unto thy servants, and thy glory unto their children.*

17   *And let the beauty of the LORD our God be upon us: and establish thou the work of our hands upon us; yea, the work of our hands establish thou it.*

~~~~~~~~~~ *** ~~~~~~~~~~

Psalm 116 - Easing the fear of death

Sometimes the fear of the unknown overwhelms us. Let the light and warmth of God surround and reassure you that the moment of transition is something to welcome.

Day: All
Candle: 7 Day-White Spiritual/Divinity

Light the candle and place near center of home. Read verses whenever feel the need. So mote it be.

Psalm 116 v 1-7

1   *I love the LORD, because he hath heard my voice and my supplications.*

2   *Because he hath inclined his ear unto me, therefore will I call upon him as long as I live.*

3   *The sorrows of death compassed me, and the pains of hell gat hold upon me: I found trouble and sorrow.*

4 *Then called I upon the name of the LORD; O LORD, I beseech thee, deliver my soul.*

5 *Gracious is the LORD, and righteous; yea, our God is merciful.*

6 *The LORD preserveth the simple: I was brought low, and he helped me.*

7 *Return unto thy rest, O my soul; for the LORD hath dealt bountifully with thee.*

4

Spirits-Demons-Talisman/Dolls

For our struggle is not against flesh and blood, but against the rulers,
against the powers, against the world forces of this darkness, against
the spiritual forces of wickedness in the heavenly places.
Ephesians 6:12

For seven days they shall make atonement for the altar and purify it;
so shall they consecrate it. Ezekiel 43:26

Magickal Tidbit
Crushed old red brick from an old church sprinkled across a
doorway will stop evil forces from crossing it.

~~~~~~~~~~ *** ~~~~~~~~~~

Psalm 49 - Gaining control over a troublesome spirit
Wanting to command a spirit to leave your space? This working
is good for getting rid of dark or troublesome spirits.

Day: Full moon
Candles: Black taper-2
Oil: Do As I Say
Incense: Nutmeg powder-1 teaspoon, Frankincense powder-1
teaspoon, Orris Root powder-1, Sandalwood-2 teaspoon,
Solomon's Seal powder-1 teaspoon
Other: Seal of Solomon drawn on a piece of parchment, Sea
salt, plain parchment paper, bat's blood ink.

This is a two day working that should be started on the first
night of the full moon after midnight. 12:15 a.m. is a good time

to begin. I strongly recommend to do this working outside. Combine all incense in a small bowl, mix well. When not using mixture store in airtight container. Create a circle sprinkling sea salt while reciting "None can pass. None can harm. All must listen and obey." Place Seal of Solomon in center of circle. On top of seal place small incense burner/bowl and light half of incense mixture in it. Anoint candle with oil, place in the West in your circle and light. Walking slowly around your circle counter-clockwise recite the verse of the Psalms nine times. When finished sit near black candle in the West. Using bat's blood ink write down your command to the spirit. You can send the spirit away from you or you can send it to someone else's place. DO NOT make a request of the spirit to do anything else for you. This is not the working for that. Pinch out candle when done the first night. On the next night do the working again with a new candle. When done with working on second night take Seal of Solomon paper with other parchment you wrote on and fold together and both black candles; bury in the west end of the oldest graveyard you can find. So mote it be.

Psalm 49 v 14

Like sheep they are laid in the grave; death shall feed on them; and the upright shall have dominion over them in the morning; and their beauty shall consume in the grave from their dwelling.

~~~~~~~~~~ *** ~~~~~~~~~~

Psalm 68 - Driving evil spirits away

This working is inspired by the most popular of all the Voodoo Queens, Marie Laveau. Many people swore by the success of her charms. To cleanse your area/home of all evil spirits use this working.

Day: New Moon
Herb: Angelica Powder
Other: 2 silver forks, red string/yarn

Sprinkle powder in corners of all rooms in the house while repeating the verse of the Psalm. Sprinkle powder across all outside entry doors of house again repeating verse. Cross forks making a cross, bind with string. Hang forks inside house above entry door people use most to come inside house. For personal protection carry a small red cotton bag with Angelica Powder whenever you leave your house. So mote it be.

Psalm 68 v 2

As smoke is driven away, so drive them away: as wax melteth before the fire, so let the wicked perish at the presence of God.

~~~~~~~~~~ *** ~~~~~~~~~~

Psalm 145 - Driving away a ghost or evil spirit

Surround yourself and love ones with the Protection of God. Fill every dark corner and hiding space with the Light of God. Let no dark or evil energy take control.

Day: All
Incense: Dried Sage bundle
Herb-Orris Root: 3 tablespoons, Wahoo Bark-2 tablespoons
Candle-7 Day: John the Conqueror & House Blessing
Other: Crushed red brick

Light Sage and smudge (let smoke lightly fill the area) all corners in the house while saying first 3 verses of Psalm aloud in each room of house. Next light the candle and place as close to center of house as possible while saying verse 13 aloud three times. Mix herbs together. Lightly sprinkle in all corners of the house while saying verses 17 & 18 aloud in each room. Sprinkle crushed red brick across all doorways while saying verses 20 & 21 aloud. Let candle burn completely out. So mote it be.

Psalm 145 v 1-2-3-13-17-18-20-21

1   *I will extol thee, my God, O king; and I will bless thy name forever and ever.*

2   *Every day will I bless thee; and I will praise thy name forever and ever.*

3   *Great is the LORD, and greatly to be praised; and his greatness is unsearchable.*

13   *Thy kingdom is an everlasting kingdom, and thy dominion endures throughout all generations.*

17   *The LORD is righteous in all his ways, and holy in all his works.*

18   *The LORD is nigh unto all them that call upon him, to all that call upon him in truth.*

20   *The LORD preserves all them that love him: but all the wicked will he destroy.*

21   *My mouth shall speak the praise of the LORD: and let all flesh bless his holy name forever and ever.*

~~~~~~~~~~ *** ~~~~~~~~~~

Psalm 33 - Banishing demons

Dark shadows in the corners? Seeing movement out of the corner of your eye? Use this prayer for protection and to send evil energies away.

Day: All
Herb: Dried Sage-loose or bundle
Oil: Protection
Other: Sea salt

In each room of house burn sage and say aloud verses. Sprinkle sea salt lightly across all doors and windows, each time ending with "In the light I do stand". So mote it be.

Psalm 33 v 20-21-22

20 *Our soul waited for the LORD: he is our help and our shield.*

21 *For our heart shall rejoice in him, because we have trusted in his holy name.*

22 *Let thy mercy, O LORD, be upon us, according as we hope in thee.*

~~~~~~~~~~ *** ~~~~~~~~~~

Psalm 104 - Repelling demons

Evil and darkness is everywhere, sitting in corners, waiting. When you know darkness is wanting to surround and destroy you use this working to keep evil away.

Day: All
Herb: Angelica Powder
Other: Parchment paper, small red flannel/cotton bag

On parchment paper write verse. Place paper and approx. 2 teaspoons Angelica Powder in red bag and tie shut. Keep with you at all times. Sprinkle Angelica Powder in the corners of all rooms in your house. So mote it be.

Psalm 104 v 35

Let the sinners be consumed out of the earth, and let the wicked be no more. Bless thou the LORD, O my soul. Praise ye the LORD.

~~~~~~~~~~ *** ~~~~~~~~~~

Psalm 52 - Preparing a hexing doll

Use this hexing charm only if someone is trying to harm you. It will bring destruction and dishonor to whoever is responsible for trying to hurt you. This working must be done exactly as stated.

Day: All
Incense: Myrrh, Crossing powder
Herb: Witch Grass
Candle: 7 Day- Black Hexing
Oil: Black Arts
Other: Parchment paper, Four Thieves Vinegar, Dove's Blood ink, black cloth doll (Items to put inside doll (only 1 or 2 items are needed)-picture of person and/or hair, nail clippings, dirt from the ground where they have stepped/their footprint, piece of cloth from clothing they have worn, small personal item(s) hair clip etc.)

Put vinegar in shallow bowl and soak parchment paper for several minutes (approx.4-6). Take out paper and let dry. When ready make sure you have cleansed your work area thoroughly. Combine equal parts Myrrh and Crossing powder. Burn mixture. Anoint candle with black arts oil and light. Anoint doll and corners of parchment paper with black arts oil as well. While doing repeat aloud "Foul and filth shall surround you. Destruction and aching you shall reap." Write person's name five times on both sides of paper for a total of ten times. Crumble paper into a small ball and place inside doll. Add other items you have to inside of doll. Fill rest of inside doll with Witches' Grass herb. Sew/pin doll shut while again saying the above words. When done sit in front of candle and hold doll with both hands while saying the verses of the Psalm. Next bury doll in a place no one will find. Place doll in hole, spit upon it several times then cover with dirt. Don't look back when leaving. Do not speak of what you have done to anyone. So mote it be.

Psalm 52

1   Why boastest thou thyself in mischief, O mighty man? the goodness of God endureth continually.

2   Thy tongue deviseth mischiefs; like a sharp razor, working deceitfully.

3   Thou lovest evil more than good; and lying rather than to speak righteousness. Selah.

4   Thou lovest all devouring words, O thou deceitful tongue.

5   God shall likewise destroy thee forever, he shall take thee away, and pluck thee out of thy dwelling place, and root thee out of the land of the living. Selah.

6   The righteous also shall see, and fear, and shall laugh at him:

7   Lo, this is the man that made not God his strength; but trusted in the abundance of his riches, and strengthened himself in his wickedness.

8   But I am like a green olive tree in the house of God: I trust in the mercy of God forever and ever.

9   I will praise thee forever, because thou hast done it: and I will wait on thy name; for it is good before thy saints.

**Dolls can be used for many purposes. The color of the doll is very important and determines what it is used for. Black-hexed & curses; Green- luck, money, gambling; Pink- success, attraction, happiness; Red- love, sex, romance; White- peace, tranquility, healing; Yellow- dispel evil, drawing friendship

~~~~~~~~~~ *** ~~~~~~~~~~

Psalm 86 - Blessing a talisman/seal/amulet

When using a magickal item in a working you want to cleanse and bless it beforehand. This is very important to insure there are no influences or energies on the talisman that you do not want or need. Do not trust someone else to do this for you.

Day: Full Moon
Incense: Sage (Fresh Dried/Bundled)
Oil: Divinity
Candles: Taper-Black & White
Other: Holy Water, Sea Salt

Best to do this working outside and as close to midnight as you can. Light sage bundle and cleanse space thoroughly. Next wash candles and amulet with Holy Water then anoint with Divinity oil. Place black and white candles side by side with amulet between them. Use sea salt and make a small circle around candles. Again use sage bundle and make sure smoke goes across circle and over candles and amulet. Light the black candle and say verses of Psalm aloud. Light the white candle and again say verses of the Psalm aloud. Again use sage bundle over candles and amulet. When feel ready pinch out candles and wipe salt circle away with your hand. Bury/destroy candles, do not use again. Your amulet is now blessed and ready. So mote it be.

Psalm 86 v 1-5 & 17

1   Bow down thine ear, O LORD, hear me: for I am poor and
    needy.
2   Preserve my soul; for I am holy: O thou my God, save thy
    servant that trusteth in thee.
3   Be merciful unto me, O Lord: for I cry unto thee daily.
4   Rejoice the soul of thy servant: for unto thee, O Lord, do I lift
    up my soul.
5   For thou, Lord, art good, and ready to forgive; and plenteous in
    mercy unto all them that call upon thee.
17 Show me a token for good; that they which hate me may see
    it, and be ashamed: because thou, LORD, hast helped me, and
    comforted me.

~~~~~~~~~~ *** ~~~~~~~~~~

Psalm 121 - Powerful protection talisman for mojo bag

When putting together a mojo/gris-gris bag one of the most important items to put in it is a protection talisman. This working will create a very powerful blessed talisman. Once blessed the talisman can also be used alone for personal protection.

Day: All
Incense: 3 Kings
Candle: Taper-White
Oil: Divine Savior
Other: Seal of Assistance or glass evil eye (this can be any size)

This working needs to be done between 11pm and midnight. Burn incense. Anoint self, candle and talisman with oil. Light the candle and say verses of Psalm aloud. When finished place talisman in front of candle and say verses aloud again. Take talisman in both hands and say three times-'Blessed am I. Protected am I from all harm and evil intent. The Lord is always with me.' Place talisman in mojo bag. Pinch out candle. Let no one touch your talisman or mojo bag. So mote it be.

Psalm 121 v 1-8

1   *I will lift up mine eyes unto the hills, from whence cometh my help.*

2   *My help cometh from the LORD, which made heaven and earth.*

3   *He will not suffer thy foot to be moved: he that keepeth thee will not slumber.*

4   *Behold, he that keepeth Israel shall neither slumber nor sleep.*

5   *The LORD is thy keeper: the LORD is thy shade upon thy right hand.*

6   *The sun shall not smite thee by day, nor the moon by night.*

7   *The LORD shall preserve thee from all evil: he shall preserve thy soul.*

8   *The LORD shall preserve thy going out and thy coming in from this time forth, and even for evermore.*

5

Enemies-Curses-Protection

"The eternal God is a dwelling place, and underneath are the everlasting arms; And He drove out the enemy from before you, And said, 'Destroy!' Deuteronomy 33:27

So do not fear, for I am with you; do not be dismayed, for I am your God. I will strengthen you and help you; I will uphold you with my righteous right hand. Isaiah 41:10

Magickal Tidbit
Never look back when leaving a cemetery/graveyard. To do so is to attract bad spirits to you.

~~~~~~~~~~ *** ~~~~~~~~~~

Psalm 18 - Keeping your enemies away from you
When needing help to keep your enemies as far as possible from you. Very effective OSY charm. The magickal word "osy" is good for protection type amulets as well.

Day: Wednesday
Incense: Camphor & Angelica
Candle: Taper –Red
Other: Dove's blood ink, parchment paper-best done after the sun sets

Light incense and candle in your sacred place. Write your enemies name in either your blood or dove's blood ink on the parchment paper three times. On other side of paper write "OSY" nine times. Place paper under candle. Say Psalm verses aloud three times.

Pinch out candle. Spit three times on names on paper then fold paper three times while saying "Three times three you will stay away from me". Bury near the gate of a graveyard. So mote it be.

Psalms 18 v 1-3

1   *I will love thee, O LORD, my strength.*

2   *The LORD is my rock, and my fortress, and my deliverer; my God, my strength, in whom I will trust; my buckler, and the horn of my salvation, and my high tower.*

3   *I will call upon the LORD, who is worthy to be praised: so shall I be saved from mine enemies.*

~~~~~~~~~~ *** ~~~~~~~~~~

Psalm 21 - Revealing your enemies

Use when you are wanting to find out if someone is working against you. Also can be used to reveal secrets that are being kept about you.

Day: Wednesday or Sunday
Incense: Camphor & Benzoin
Oil: Dragon's Blood
Candle: Taper-Black
Other: Parchment paper, mirror, small knife

This working is best done after the sun sets. Anoint candle with Dragon's Blood oil. Place blank parchment paper under candle in front of mirror. Sit in front of mirror, light the candle and recite verses slowly and with purpose. Afterwards sit quietly and look into mirror for several minutes. Pinch out candle and do not use again. Remove paper from under candle and wrap around blade of knife. Put knife in a safe secret place. Soon all will be revealed. Later when done burn paper-do not reuse for other purposes. Cleanse knife blade with holy water.

Psalm 21 v 8-13

8   *Thine hand shall find out all thine enemies: thy right hand shall find out those that hate thee.*

9   *Thou shalt make them as a fiery oven in the time of thine anger: the LORD shall swallow them up in his wrath, and the fire shall devour them.*

10   *Their fruit shalt thou destroy from the earth, and their seed from among the children of men.*

11   *For they intended evil against thee: they imagined a mischievous device, which they are not able to perform.*

12   *Therefore shalt thou make them turn their back, when thou shalt make ready thine arrows upon thy strings against the face of them.*

13   *Be thou exalted, LORD, in thine own strength: so will we sing and praise thy power.*

~~~~~~~~~~ *** ~~~~~~~~~~

Psalm 92 – Revealing Enemies' Plans

When you know that plans are being made against you this working will reveal all that is being plotted. This is a good working to use for when you are not sure who the enemy is.

Day: Full Moon
Incense: (All powder) Rose-1/4 cup, Sandalwood-1/4 cup, Frankincense-1/4 cup, Cinnamon-2 tablespoons, Orris-2 tablespoons, Wormwood-1 tablespoon, Saltpeter-pinch, Orchid-1 tablespoon
Oil: Psychic
Candle: Black taper
Herb: Queen Elizabeth root
Other-parchment paper-full sheet, Dove's Blood ink, small red cotton bag, red thread/string

Combine incense mixture and store in airtight container. This working should be done on the first night of the full moon between midnight and 1 a.m. Start by burning couple tablespoons of incense mixture. Next anoint candle, Queen Elizabeth root and red cotton bag with oil. Using Dove's blood ink write verse 11 in center of parchment paper. On other side draw a large eye in center and then a cross in each corner of paper. Anoint center of crosses with oil. Fold the paper as small as can make and place in red cotton bag along with Queen Elizabeth root. Sprinkle a little of incense mixture in bag and tie securely shut using red thread/ string. Holding bag with both hands say verses of Psalm aloud several times building energy. When you feel ready place bag beside candle and sit quietly concentrating on what you want to know. When done pinch out candle and throw in moving waters. Place bag somewhere safe until done then destroy. During the next moon cycle all will be revealed to you. So mote it be.

Psalm 92 v 11-15

11   *Mine eye also shall see my desire on mine enemies, and mine ears shall hear my desire of the wicked that rise up against me.*

12   *The righteous shall flourish like the palm tree: he shall grow like a cedar in Lebanon.*

13   *Those that be planted in the house of the LORD shall flourish in the courts of our God.*

14   *They shall still bring forth fruit in old age; they shall be fat and flourishing;*

15   *To show that the LORD is upright: he is my rock, and there is no unrighteousness in him.*

~~~~~~~~~~ *** ~~~~~~~~~~

Psalm 31 - Reversing plots against you

Send the evil doers' deeds back to them. All that they wished against you will be brought upon them. This is a good working to do if you are not sure of exactly who the person is.

Day: All
Candles: Taper- Black & Red
Oil: Reversing
Other: red cloth/handkerchief

Rub oil all over black and red candles while saying "In the light of Divinity I ask this deed to be done". Place candles side by side, light the red candle and say all the verses. Light black candle and repeat three times "What thou gives thou haves." Let candles burn until completely done. Take wax and wrap tightly using string/thread in red cloth while saying all verses. Throw bag in a river. Once done turn and don't look back. So mote it be.

Psalm 31 v 4-5-17-18-23-24

4   *Pull me out of the net that they have laid privily for me: for thou art my strength.*

5   *Into thine hand I commit my spirit: thou hast redeemed me, O LORD God of truth.*

17   *Let me not be ashamed, O LORD; for I have called upon thee: let the wicked be ashamed, and let them be silent in the grave.*

18   *Let the lying lips be put to silence; which speak grievous things proudly and contemptuously against the righteous.*

23   *O love the LORD, all ye his saints: for the LORD preserveth the faithful, and plentifully rewardeth the proud doer.*

24   *Be of good courage, and he shall strengthen your heart, all ye that hope in the LORD.*

~~~~~~~~~~ *** ~~~~~~~~~~

Psalm 54 - Destroying one's enemies

This is a very powerful working that should only be done after careful consideration. Once done it cannot be undone. It is a blood curse and will affect the family of the cursed one for generations to come.

Day: All
Incense: Black Arts
Oil: Crossing
Candle: Taper-Black
Other: Seal of Mephistophilis, Dove's Blood ink or your own blood.

Burn incense. Anoint candle with crossing oil. While reading aloud the Psalms do the following: verse 2- light black candle, verse 3- write down name/s using Dove's Blood ink or your own blood across the Seal three times, verse 4- fold paper three times, verse 6- burn paper in candle flame. Pinch out candle and throw it away or bury it. Do NOT light the candle again. So mote it be.

Psalm 54

1   *Save me, O God, by thy name, and judge me by thy strength.*

2   *Hear my prayer, O God; give ear to the words of my mouth.*

3   *For strangers are risen up against me, and oppressors seek after my soul: they have not set God before them. Selah.*

4   *Behold, God is mine helper: the Lord is with them that uphold my soul.*

5   *He shall reward evil unto mine enemies: cut them off in thy truth.*

6   *I will freely sacrifice unto thee: I will praise thy name, O LORD; for it is good.*

7   *For he hath delivered me out of all trouble: and mine eye hath seen his desire upon mine enemies.*

~~~~~~~~~~ ***** ~~~~~~~~~~

Psalm 55 - Dividing your enemies

Sometimes the best plan of action is to divide your enemies and let them destroy each other.

Day: Wednesday, after midnight
Candle: Black taper
Oil: Confusion & Conquering (equal amounts)
Herb: Flax seed & Black mustard seed-2 tablespoon each
Other: Graveyard dirt-2 tablespoons, glass jar with lid, small square of red cloth (approx. 6"x6"), white cornmeal, spring water, white thread/string/yarn, parchment paper, Dove's blood ink

Anoint candle, jar and corners of cloth with equal amounts of Confusion & Conquering oil. Mix together Flax seed, Black Mustard seed & Graveyard dirt. Put mixture in jar. Write down verses of Psalm on parchment paper using Dove's blood ink. Fold paper and place in jar. Fill rest of jar with spring water. Close jar tightly. Cover jar lid with cloth and secure with white thread. Using the white cornmeal draw the sign of the cross on the cloth on top of the jar. While holding the jar in your hands say the verses of the Psalm aloud with deep emotion and intent. Repeat two more times for a total of three times. Hide jar in a secret place that cannot be found. So mote it be.

Psalm 55 v 1-9

1   *Give ear to my prayer, O God; and hide not thyself from my supplication.*
2   *Attend unto me, and hear me: I mourn in my complaint, and make a noise;*
3   *Because of the voice of the enemy, because of the oppression of the wicked: for they cast iniquity upon me, and in wrath they hate me.*
4   *My heart is sore pained within me: and the terrors of death are*

fallen upon me.

5 *Fearfulness and trembling are come upon me, and horror hath overwhelmed me.*

6 *And I said, Oh that I had wings like a dove! For then would I fly away, and be at rest.*

7 *Lo, then would I wander far off, and remain in the wilderness. Selah.*

8 *I would hasten my escape from the windy storm and tempest.*

9 *Destroy, O Lord, and divide their tongues: for I have seen violence and strife in the city.*

~~~~~~~~~~ *** ~~~~~~~~~~

Psalm 59 - Asking God to judge your enemies

Give unto God your enemies for He will judge them accordingly and righteously. When you are completely innocent of any wrongdoing and can "stand as an upright man" then use this working without creating any negativity around you.

An upright man as defined in the Bible is someone who has taken the Holy Spirit within them and strives to live within the light of Divinity.

Day: All
Candle: Double Action Reverse-black
Other: Parchment paper, Dove's Blood ink, 57 cents (shiny, new-2 quarters, 1 nickel, 2 pennies)

Write person's name nine times on parchment paper using Dove's Blood ink. Place paper under candle and light the candle. Say verses of Psalm aloud. Let candle burn completely (approx. seven days) out then take paper and burn it. Scatter ashes in a cemetery/graveyard. When leaving the graveyard place the 57 cents on grave closest to the exit. Leave, don't look back. So mote it be.

Psalm 59 v 9-17

9   Because of his strength will I wait upon thee: for God is my
    defense.

10 The God of my mercy shall prevent me: God shall let me see my
    desire upon mine enemies.

11 Slay them not, lest my people forget: scatter them by thy power;
    and bring them down, O Lord our shield.

12 For the sin of their mouth and the words of their lips let them
    even be taken in their pride: and for cursing and lying which
    they speak.

13 Consume them in wrath, consume them, that they may not be:
    and let them know that God ruleth in Jacob unto the ends of the
    earth. Selah.

14 And at evening let them return; and let them make a noise like
    a dog, and go round about the city.

15 Let them wander up and down for meat, and grudge if they be
    not satisfied.

16 But I will sing of thy power; yea, I will sing aloud of thy mercy
    in the morning: for thou hast been my defense and refuge in the
    day of my trouble.

17 Unto thee, O my strength, will I sing: for God is my defense,
    and the God of my mercy.

~~~~~~~~~~ *** ~~~~~~~~~~

Psalm 83 - Asking God to judge your enemies

Don't lower yourself to the actions of others. This working is
really good for when you know that your enemies have lied or
acted in a false matter. Let the wrath of God come down upon
those who deserve it.

Day: All
Incense: Sandalwood-1\2 cup, Solomon's Seal powder-2
teaspoons, Wormwood-2 tablespoons

Candle: 7 Day-Black Double Action
Other: Seal of Solomon, 2 cups Solomon's Seal powder, parchment paper, Dove's blood ink, graveyard dirt

Combine incense ingredients and store in airtight container. This working needs to start right after midnight. Using Solomon's Seal powder make a small circle. Place Seal of Solomon in center of circle with candle. Put 4 small dishes of incense mixture in cardinal points (east, south, west, north) around outside of circle. Burn incense and light the candle. Read verses of Psalm aloud once. Write enemies name(s) on parchment using Dove's ink blood. Place parchment paper under candle in center of circle. Slowly walk counter-clockwise around outside of circle three times while saying aloud at each cardinal point the following- "God is just. God is righteous." You want to build the intensity and energy each time you say it. At the end you should almost be shouting with deep emotion. After candle has burned completely out (approx. 6-7 days) take Seal of Solomon and parchment paper with name/s on it and fold together several times and bury in a graveyard. So mote it be.

Psalm 83 v 13-18

13 *O my God, make them like a wheel; the stubble before the wind.*

14 *As the fire burneth a wood, and as the flame setteth the mountains on fire;*

15 *So persecute them with thy tempest, and make them afraid with thy storm.*

16 *Fill their faces with shame; that they may seek thy name, O LORD.*

17 *Let them be confounded and troubled forever; yea, let them be put to shame, and perish:*

18 *That men may know that thou, whose name alone is JEHOVAH, art the most high over all the earth.*

~~~~~~~~~~ *** ~~~~~~~~~~

Psalm 94 - Stopping a bitter enemy

Some people just can't stop and never let go of the past. When you have to deal with this type of person this working will aid you in keeping them from continuing to try to hurt or destroy you.

Day: Monday
Incense: Black Arts-1 teaspoon, Myrrh-1 teaspoon, Dragon's Blood powder-1 teaspoon, Poke Root Powder-1 teaspoon
Candle: 7 Day-Black
Other: black doll prepared in likeness of person (Psalm 52 working), parchment paper, Dragon's blood ink, Graveyard dirt (handful)

Best to do this working on a Monday closest to Full moon after midnight. Combine incense mixture and burn. Write verses on Psalm on parchment paper using Dragon's blood ink. Wrap doll in paper and secure with string\rubber band. Light the candle and say verses of Psalms aloud. Lay doll beside candle and walk three circles around it sprinkling graveyard dirt on the doll. Carefully pick up doll without touching it (use tongs or two sticks). Take doll to a crossroad and bury in hole nearby. Throw out any remaining incense mixture. Speak to no one of what you have done. So mote it be.

Psalm 94 v 1-2, 20-23

1   *O LORD God, to whom vengeance belongeth; O God, to whom vengeance belongeth show thyself.*
2   *Lift up thyself, thou judge of the earth: render a reward to the proud.*
20 *Shall the throne of iniquity have fellowship with thee, which frameth mischief by a law?*

21 *They gather themselves together against the soul of the righteous, and condemn the innocent blood.*

22 *But the LORD is my defense; and my God is the rock of my refuge.*

23 *And he shall bring upon them their own iniquity, and shall cut them off in their own wickedness; yea, the LORD our God shall cut them off.*

~~~~~~~~~~ *** ~~~~~~~~~~

Psalm 110 - Confusing your enemies

Make your enemies confused and they will act stupid causing all their plans to come crashing down.

Day: All
Incense: Chicory-2 teaspoons, Asafoetida powder-2 teaspoons, Saltpeter-pinch
Oil: Confusion, Controlling
Other: Cornmeal-approx. 2cups, parchment paper, Dove's blood ink

Best to do this working outside as it requires spreading cornmeal around. On parchment write your enemies names using Dove's Blood ink. Dab each name with both Confusion and Controling oils. Fold paper in half with names facing inwards. On outside of paper write verse 1 of the Psalm down using Dove's Blood ink. Using cornmeal make a small circle and place paper in center. On top of paper put incense mixture and burn. When paper is ash wait for to cool then blend all with cornmeal while saying verses of Psalm aloud. Visualize your enemies scattering confused and stupid. Spread cornmeal all over the place. Throw it to the wind. So mote it be.

Psalm 110 v 1-2-3

1   *The LORD said unto my Lord, Sit thou at my right hand, until I make thine enemies thy footstool.*

2   *The LORD shall send the rod of thy strength out of Zion: rule thou in the midst of thine enemies.*

3   *Thy people shall be willing in the day of thy power, in the beauties of holiness from the womb of the morning: thou hast the dew of thy youth.*

~~~~~~~~~~ *** ~~~~~~~~~~

Psalm 125 - Keeping enemies from harming you

This working can only be used by an 'upright and just' person-meaning you have nothing wrong and have not tried to retaliate or get back at the person/s trying to hurt/harm you. Very effective if done correctly.

Day: Wednesday
Herb: Barberry, Rue, Black Mustard Seed, Black Salt-equal amounts, approx. ½ tablespoon each
Oil: Keep Away Enemies
Other: Graveyard dirt-small handful, red cotton/flannel bag, white string

Blend all herbs together with graveyard dirt and place in bag. Secure with white string and anoint bag with oil. Hold bag with both hands and say aloud the verses of the Psalm nine times. Afterwards anoint self with oil. Keep bag in a safe place. To insure success do acts of charity or kindness whenever possible. So mote it be.

Psalm 125 v 1-2-3

1   *They that trust in the LORD shall be as mount Zion, which cannot be removed, but abideth forever.*

2   As the mountains are round about Jerusalem, so the LORD is round about his people from henceforth even forever.

3   For the rod of the wicked shall not rest upon the lot of the righteous; lest the righteous put forth their hands unto iniquity.

~~~~~~~~~~ *** ~~~~~~~~~~

Psalm 7 - Stopping a curse or hex

When you know you have been cursed this prayer will stop it and send the energy back to the person who did it. Very powerful and should only be used when you know for sure who the person is.

Day: Wednesday
Incense: Camphor
Candle: Taper- Black
Other: Parchment paper, picture or personal item of person who cursed you, sea salt, red cotton or flannel bag

Light incense. On one side of paper write the word "Justice". On other side of paper write the person's name. Light the candle and while saying the verses light paper from candle and let burn completely. Take the ashes and personal item and put them in the bag. Take outside and bury close to a crossroads. You can pinch out candle after or let burn. Lightly sprinkle sea salt across all doors and windows in your house. So mote it be.

Psalm 7 v 1- 6- 16

1   O LORD my God, in thee do I put my trust: save me from all them that persecute me, and deliver me:

6   Arise, O LORD, in thine anger, lift up thyself because of the rage of mine enemies: and awake for me to the judgment that thou hast commanded.

16   His mischief shall return upon his own head, and his violent dealing shall come down upon his own plate.

~~~~~~~~~~ *** ~~~~~~~~~~

Psalm 35 - Returning a curse to sender

This is Papa Nico's favorite for dealing with curses. When you know that someone has put a curse on you this working will send all that negativity back to them. You must know the name of the person and know for certain it was them. If any doubts about who the person is, use the 'Reversing plots against You-Psalm 31' working instead.

Day: All
Candle: 7 Day-Red & Black
Incense: Myrrh
Oil: Revenge
Other: Parchment paper

Burn incense. Write person's name on piece of parchment, fold in half. Place three drops of oil inside edges of both candles. Place candles side by side and put paper with person's name under the black candle. While reading the verses aloud do the following-verse 1 light red candle, verse 4 light black candle. When done reading verses take paper and light with black candle, let paper completely burn to ash. Take ashes outside and place in pile on dirt. Place your heel on top of ash pile and grind into the ground while saying "Ashes to ashes, dirt to dirt, all that you gave is now yours." Say several times until you feel satisfied. Turn and walk away, don't look back at where ash pile was. Let candles burn until completely out-about seven days. So mote it be.

Psalm 35 v 1-9

1   *Plead my cause, O LORD, with them that strive with me: fight against them that fight against me.*

2   *Take hold of shield and buckler, and stand up for mine help.*

3   *Draw out also the spear, and stop the way against them that*

persecute me: say unto my soul, I am thy salvation.

4   *Let them be confounded and put to shame that seek after my soul: let them be turned back and brought to confusion that devise my hurt.*

5   *Let them be as chaff before the wind: and let the angel of the LORD chase them.*

6   *Let their way be dark and slippery: and let the angel of the LORD persecute them.*

7   *For without cause have they hid for me their net in a pit, which without cause they have digged for my soul.*

8   *Let destruction come upon him at unawares; and let his net that he hath hid catch himself: into that very destruction let him fall.*

9   *And my soul shall be joyful in the LORD: it shall rejoice in his salvation.*

~~~~~~~~~~ *** ~~~~~~~~~~

Psalm 109 - Cursing someone who has wronged you

"Three times three their crime will return to them." Call upon the dogs of hell to bite at their heels with this dark and deadly curse. Use only after very careful consideration. This working is one of the best examples in the use of numerology and hidden text lines.

Day: All
Incense: Asafoetida-1/2 teaspoon, Crossing powder-2 tablespoons, Dragon's Blood powder-2 teaspoons, saltpeter-1/2 teaspoon
Oil: Obeah
Other: Photograph of person, parchment paper, Dove's Blood ink, hair of enemy (if possible)

Mix incense ingredients together. Write person's name using Dove's Blood ink on parchment paper. Across name write the following-'Three times three your crime will return to thee'. On corners of paper dab Obeah oil. Place photograph on small white dish. Atop place parchment paper and person's hair. Pour incense mixture on top of parchment and light. While it is burning say verses of Psalm aloud. Let ashes cool and scatter outside after midnight. So mote it be.

Psalm 109 v 1-2-3-7-8-9-13-14-15-19-20-21-25-26-27-31

1   *Hold not thy peace, O God of my praise;*

2   *For the mouth of the wicked and the mouth of the deceitful are opened against me: they have spoken against me with a lying tongue.*

3   *They compassed me about also with words of hatred; and fought against me without a cause.*

7   *When he shall be judged, let him be condemned: and let his prayer become sin.*

8   *Let his days be few; and let another take his office.*

9   *Let his children be fatherless, and his wife a widow.*

13   *Let his posterity be cut off; and in the generation following let their name be blotted out.*

14   *Let the iniquity of his fathers be remembered with the LORD; and let not the sin of his mother be blotted out.*

15   *Let them be before the LORD continually, that he may cut off the memory of them from the earth.*

19   *Let it be unto him as the garment which covereth him, and for a girdle wherewith he is girded continually.*

20   *Let this be the reward of mine adversaries from the LORD, and of them that speak evil against my soul.*

21   *But do thou for me, O GOD the Lord, for thy name's sake: because thy mercy is good, deliver thou me.*

25   *I became also a reproach unto them: when they looked upon me they shaked their heads.*

26   *Help me, O LORD my God: O save me according to thy mercy:*

27   *That they may know that this is thy hand; that thou, LORD, hast done it.*

31   *For he shall stand at the right hand of the poor, to save him from*
     those that condemn his soul.

~ ~ ~ ~ ~ ~ ~ ~ ~ ~ ******* ~ ~ ~ ~ ~ ~ ~ ~ ~ ~

Psalm 109 - Stopping someone from doing evil against you

This working will bring failure to anyone's attempts to work dark/evil negative energies against you. If done correctly it is very powerful. Does not send anything back to evil doer only causes their work to fail. Good to use if you do not want to hurt the person.

Day: Sunday
Candles: Taper-Black& White
Oil: High Conquering
Incense: Patchouli- 1 teaspoon, Ruda powder-1 teaspoon Bayberry-1/2 teaspoon, Saltpeter-pinch, Tonka beans (crushed)-1/4 cup, Jasmine-1/4 cup
Other: Sea salt

Do this working before midnight. Blend all incense ingredients together and store in airtight container. Before starting take a bath with six drops of High Conquering oil added. When ready prepare space you are doing the working in by thoroughly cleansing/smudging. Lightly sprinkle sea salt in area. Burn 2 tablespoons of incense mixture. Hold black candle in your hands and say verses of Psalm aloud. Next take white candle in your hands and say aloud three times- "In the Light of Divinity I will receive thee. Bless me my Lord. Bless my enemies my Lord". Anoint both candles with High Conquering oil. Place candles side by side and light. Sit in front of candles and again read verses of Psalm aloud this time thinking about peace, resolution, happiness in you and your families' lives. When finished pinch out candles and do not reuse. Best to bury them together near the entry to a graveyard or cemetery on the next full moon. Continue to burn incense daily until get desired effect. So mote it be.

Psalm 109 v 26-31

26 *Help me, O LORD my God: O save me according to thy mercy:*
27 *That they may know that this is thy hand; that thou, LORD, hast done it.*
28 *Let them curse, but bless thou: when they arise, let them be ashamed; but let thy servant rejoice.*
29 *Let mine adversaries be clothed with shame, and let them cover themselves with their own confusion, as with a mantle.*
30 *I will greatly praise the LORD with my mouth; yea, I will praise him among the multitude.*
31 *For he shall stand at the right hand of the poor, to save him from those that condemn his soul.*

~~~~~~~~~~ ***** ~~~~~~~~~~

Psalm 71 - Breaking up with a cruel man/woman
When safety and protection are needed in ending a relationship this working will aide you.

Day: All
Incense: Helping hand
Herb: Low John the Conqueror Root
Oil: Peace, Go Away
Other: Parchment paper, red thread/string

Set up a space that this working can stay undisturbed for seven days. Burn Helping hand incense. Anoint root with equal amounts of peace and go away oils while saying verses. On parchment paper write verse 4 (if subject is a woman write that where the word 'man' is). Wrap parchment around root and secure with red thread. For next six days, each morning burn a little helping hand incense. Hold root in hands and say all verses aloud. On seventh day take root and bury where cruel person will walk over it. So mote it be.

Psalm 71 v 2-3-4-5

2   *Deliver me in thy righteousness, and cause me to escape: incline thine ear unto me, and save me.*

3   *Be thou my strong habitation, whereunto I may continually resort: thou hast given commandment to save me; for thou art my rock and my fortress.*

4   *Deliver me, O my God, out of the hand of the wicked, out of the hand of the unrighteous and cruel man.*

5   *For thou art my hope, O Lord God: thou art my trust from my youth.*

~~~~~~~~~~ *** ~~~~~~~~~~

Psalm 51 – Self Protection

Said to ward off all forms of evil, this working is inspired by Marie Laveau, who swore by the power of Angelica Powder (Orris Root).

Day: All
Incense: Go Away Evil
Herb: Hyssop-2 tablespoons, Angelica Powder-4 tablespoons
Other: Red flannel or cotton bag, parchment paper

Light incense. Combine Hyssop and 2 tablespoons Angelica Powder, place in red bag. Upon the parchment paper write your full name nine times. Fold paper three times, put in bag and tie securely shut. Hold bag in your hands and say the verses of the Psalm. Keep bag on your person or in your space. Take remaining Angelica Powder and sprinkle in all corners of your bedroom. So mote it be.

Psalm 51 v 7- 10- 11- 12

7   *Purge me with hyssop, and I shall be clean: wash me, and I shall be whiter than snow.*

10 *Create in me a clean heart, O God; and renew a right spirit within me.*

11 *Cast me not away from thy presence; and take not thy holy spirit from me.*

12 *Restore unto me the joy of thy salvation; and uphold me with thy free spirit.*

~~~~~~~~~~ *** ~~~~~~~~~~

Psalm 89 - Protection

Use this working for protection in your daily life. Very good for when you know you are meeting new people and unsure of their intent towards you.

Day: All
Incense: Uncrossing powder, Helping Hand powder- equal amounts
Candle: 7 Day-White Protection
Other: Lodestone

This is a three day working that should be done early in the morning each day.

One the first morning burn incense and light the candle. Sit quietly in front of candle holding lodestone in your hands. Say verses aloud three times. Place lodestone beside candle. Next morning burn more incense and repeat verses holding lodestone in your hands. Repeat again on the third day. Afterwards let candle burn completely out. Keep lodestone with you at all times. So mote it be.

Psalm 89 v 13- 14- 15

13 *Thou hast a mighty arm: strong is thy hand, and high is thy right hand.*

14 Justice and judgment are the habitation of thy throne: mercy and truth shall go before thy face.

15 Blessed is the people that know the joyful sound: they shall walk, O LORD, in the light of thy countenance.

~~~~~~~~~~ *** ~~~~~~~~~~

Psalm 91 - Protection

One of the most popular Psalms in use today for protection workings. This is another favorite of Papa Nico to be used when you know evil is near.

Day: All

Read Psalm aloud changing the word 'thee/thou' to 'me/I' whenever you feel the presence of evil is near. So mote it be.

Psalm 91

1   *He that dwelleth in the secret place of the most High shall abide under the shadow of the Almighty.*

2   *I will say of the LORD, He is my refuge and my fortress: my God; in him will I trust.*

3   *Surely he shall deliver me from the snare of the fowler, and from the noisome pestilence.*

4   *He shall cover me with his feathers, and under his wings shalt I trust: his truth shall be my shield and buckler.*

5   *I shalt not be afraid for the terror by night; nor for the arrow that flieth by day;*

6   *Nor for the pestilence that walketh in darkness; nor for the destruction that wasteth at noonday.*

7   *A thousand shall fall at my side, and ten thousand at my right*

hand; but it shall not come nigh me.

8 *Only with mine eyes shalt I behold and see the reward of the wicked.*

9 *Because I hast made the LORD, which is my refuge, even the most High, my habitation;*

10 *There shall no evil befall me, neither shall any plague come nigh my dwelling. 11 For he shall give his angels charge over me, to keep me in all thy ways.*

12 *They shall bear me up in their hands, lest I dash my foot against a stone.*

13 *I shalt tread upon the lion and adder: the young lion and the dragon shalt I trample under feet.*

14 *Because he hath set his love upon me, therefore will I deliver him: I will set him on high, because he hath known my name.*

15 *He shall call upon me, and I will answer him: I will be with him in trouble; I will deliver him, and honour him.*

16 *With long life will I satisfy him, and show him my salvation.*

6

Legal-Justice-Jail

Open your mouth for the mute, for the rights of all who are destitute. Open your mouth, judge righteously, defend the rights of the poor and needy. Proverbs 31:8-9

The Lord is not slow to fulfill his promise as some count slowness, but is patient toward you, not wishing that any should perish, but that all should reach repentance. Peter 3:9

Magickal Tidbit
Work blessings before midnight, and hexes & curses after midnight.

~~~~~~~~~~ *** ~~~~~~~~~~

Psalm 7 - Justice in Court/legal matters
Use this working when you are in the right and wanting a fair and just settlement.

Day: Sunday
Incense: John the Conqueror
Oil: Legal/Court Matters
Candle: 7 Day-Success
Other: 3 shiny pennies, holy water

This is a seven day working and is best to start the working on a Sunday if possible. The candle needs to burn for the entire seven days without putting out. On the first day, preferably at dawn, light the candle and say all verses, slowly and with purpose. Rinse three pennies with holy water and place near candle. Then wash face and hands with holy water. Do NOT put out candle. For next six days in the morning say verses and then wash face and hands with holy water. On day of court appearance put pennies in your pocket or wallet and oil on palms of your hands and the bottom of your feet. So mote it be.

Psalm 7 v.11-17

11 *God judges the righteous, and God is angry with the wicked every day.*

12 *If he turn not, he will whet his sword; he hath bent his bow, and made it ready.*

13 *He hath also prepared for him the instruments of death; he ordained his arrows against the persecutors.*

14 *Behold, he travailed with iniquity, and hath conceived mischief, and brought forth falsehood.*

15 *He made a pit, and digged it, and is fallen into the ditch which he made.*

16 *His mischief shall return upon his own head, and his violent dealing shall come down upon his own plate.*

17 *I will praise the LORD according to his righteousness: and will sing praise.*

~~~~~~~~~~ *** ~~~~~~~~~~

Psalm 26 - Staying out of jail

Use this prayer when wanting another option rather than going to jail. Remember we must all be responsible for our actions but sometimes jail is not the answer. Accept responsibility and ask for leniency.

Day: All, best on a Full Moon
Incense: John the Conqueror
Candle: 7 Day-Stay Out of Jail
Oil: Stay Out of Jail

Other: parchment paper, red thread, small fire outside or fire proof container inside

Write your full name and date of birth on parchment paper, fold paper in half three times. Wrap a red thread around paper while reading the verses. Next light the candle and incense then place dab of oil on forehead. In a fire proof container burn the paper while repeating the verses several times. Let burn completely then throw the ashes to the wind outside. Each morning while candles burns say verses and put oil on forehead. Don't worry if candle doesn't burn exactly seven days. Also do a good deed or act of charity. So mote it be.

Psalm 26 v 9-10-11

9   *Gather not my soul with sinners, nor my life with bloody men:*
10   *In whose hands is mischief, and their right hand is full of bribes.*
11   *But as for me, I will walk in mine integrity: redeem me, and be merciful unto me.*

~~~~~~~~~~ *** ~~~~~~~~~~

Psalm 46 - Unite disagreeing parties/stop quarreling

Need to bring people together, to find compromise, to let go of the past and move forward? This working will help both sides in finding peace in any situation.

Day: All, after sunset
Incense: Uncrossing
Herb: White Clover powder, Blue Vervain, Broom herb-1 teaspoon each
Candle: Taper-Yellow
Oil: Peace
Other: Parchment paper, white thread

Light the candle and incense then say aloud all verses. Write on paper "Unity, Truth, Love". On other side write names of parties involved. Place small dab of oil on all four corners of paper. Again say all verses aloud while folding paper in half as many times as can. Bind paper with white thread. Bury on the north side of a tree with herbal mixture. Pinch candle out—can be re-used for blessing works. So mote it be.

Psalm 46

1   *God is our refuge and strength, a very present help in trouble.*

2   *Therefore will not we fear, though the earth be removed, and though the mountains be carried into the midst of the sea;*

3   *Though the waters thereof roar and be troubled, though the mountains shake with the swelling thereof. Selah.*

4   *There is a river, the streams whereof shall make glad the city of God, the holy place of the tabernacles of the most High.*

5   *God is in the midst of her; she shall not be moved: God shall help her, and that right early.*

6   *The heathen raged, the kingdoms were moved: he uttered his voice, the earth melted.*

7   *The LORD of hosts is with us; the God of Jacob is our refuge. Selah.*

8   *Come, behold the works of the LORD, what desolations he hath made in the earth.*

9   *He maketh wars to cease unto the end of the earth; he breaketh the bow, and cutteth the spear in sunder; he burneth the chariot in the fire.*

10 *Be still, and know that I am God: I will be exalted among the heathen, I will be exalted in the earth.*

11 *The LORD of hosts is with us; the God of Jacob is our refuge. Selah.*

**Serve a meal including black-eyed peas and boiled rice to all parties involved.

~~~~~~~~~~ *** ~~~~~~~~~~

Psalm 94 - Being falsely accused

To bring to light the truth of the matter and for all to see your innocence use this very powerful working. Be careful for secrets long hidden may come to light and dark skeletons in closets may become known for all parties involved.

Day: All

Herbal Bath: Marigold, Lemon Verbena, Mace, Calamus, Hyssop-equal amounts.

Let herbs seep in gallon of fresh spring water for three days. Strain mixture and use ½ cup of water in bath for seven days. Each morning read the verses of the Psalm. When done throw out rest of bath mixture, do not store or use. Within three days of finishing working you should see the start of some results. If not repeat working. So mote it be.

Psalm 94 v 1-2, 12-15

1   *O LORD God, to whom vengeance belongeth; O God, to whom vengeance belongeth, show thyself.*

2   *Lift up thyself, thou judge of the earth: render a reward to the proud.*

12   *Blessed is the man whom thou chastenest, O LORD, and teachest him out of thy law;*

13   *That thou mayest give him rest from the days of adversity, until the pit be digged for the wicked.*

14   *For the LORD will not cast off his people, neither will he forsake his inheritance.*

15   *But judgment shall return unto righteousness: and all the upright in heart shall follow it.*

~~~~~~~~~~ *** ~~~~~~~~~~

Psalm 99 - Justice in legal matters

This working is for when seeking a fair and just conclusion in any legal matter. Very good for property disputes or settling a will/inheritance.

Day: All
Oil: Cassava Sagrada-1 teaspoon, Court
Candle: 7 Day-Success
Other: Parchment paper

Blend six drops Court oil and Cassava Sagrada together. Write verse 4 of the Psalm on parchment paper. Place oil mixture in center of paper and fold paper several times. Anoint candle with Court oil and light. Place parchment near candle and say verses aloud. Afterwards keep paper with you at all times until matters are settled. So mote it be.

Psalm 99 v 2-3-4

2   *The LORD is great in Zion; and he is high above all the people.*
3   *Let them praise thy great and terrible name; for it is holy.*
4   *The king's strength also loveth judgment; thou dost establish equity, thou executest judgment and righteousness in Jacob.*

~~~~~~~~~~ *** ~~~~~~~~~~

Psalm 119 - Wrongful persecution

You can call for justice and the truth to be seen by all using this very effective working. Let your innocence be known.

Day: Tuesday
Incense: John the Conqueror
Oil: Peace
Other: Four Thieves Vinegar

Burn incense. Wash hands and feet with Four Thieves Vinegar. When finished anoint self with Peace oil. Sit quietly and read verses of Psalm while concentrating on the situation. Repeat daily until get desired results. So mote it be.

Psalm 119 v 81-88

81 *My soul fainteth for thy salvation: but I hope in thy word.*

82 *Mine eyes fail for thy word, saying, When wilt thou comfort me?*

83 *For I am become like a bottle in the smoke; yet do I not forget thy statutes.*

84 *How many are the days of thy servant? when wilt thou execute judgment on them that persecute me?*

85 *The proud have digged pits for me, which are not after thy law.*

86 *All thy commandments are faithful: they persecute me wrongfully; help thou me.*

87 *They had almost consumed me upon earth; but I forsook not thy precepts.*

88 *Quicken me after thy loving kindness; so shall I keep the testimony of thy mouth.*

~~~~~~~~~~ *** ~~~~~~~~~~

Psalm 119 - Appearing before a Judge

This working is based upon a very powerful spell that Marie Laveau swore by. She said that the judge will go easy on whoever uses this working.

Day: All
Incense: John the Conqueror
Herb: Cascara Sagrada-2 teaspoons
Candle: 7 Day-Success
Oil: Court
Other: Parchment paper

Combine 1 teaspoon of Cassava Sagrada with six drops Court onto piece of parchment paper. Fold paper to secure mixture and place under your mattress seven days before seeing judge. On morning to see judge burn incense. Anoint candle with oil and light. Read verses of Psalm aloud. Take parchment paper from under mattress and keep with you when seeing judge. So mote it be.

Psalm 119 v89-96

89 *Forever, O LORD, thy word is settled in heaven.*

90 *Thy faithfulness is unto all generations: thou hast established the earth, and it abideth.*

91 *They continue this day according to thine ordinances: for all are thy servants. 92 Unless thy law had been my delights, I should then have perished in mine affliction.*

93 *I will never forget thy precepts: for with them thou hast quickened me.*

94 *I am thine, save me; for I have sought thy precepts.*

95 *The wicked have waited for me to destroy me: but I will consider thy testimonies.*

96 *I have seen an end of all perfection: but thy commandment is exceeding broad.*

~~~~~~~~~~ *** ~~~~~~~~~~

Psalm 142 - Seeking early release from prison
You can influence the Fates and change your destiny using this working. Help release papers be looked kindly upon by those with the power to change or approve them. Once done you must live your life righteously or this working could turn into a curse. Use wisely.

Day: All
Incense: Dragon's Blood powder-2 teaspoons, Doggrass-1

teaspoon
Candle: Taper-Purple
Oil: Just Judge, Road Opener
Other: Parchment paper, Dragon's Blood ink, toothpick

Mix incense ingredients together and store in airtight container. Using toothpick write person's full birth name on candle three times. Anoint candle with both oils. On parchment paper write person's full birth name and date of birth using the Dragon's Blood ink. Place candle on top of paper and light while saying verses of Psalm. Burn incense mixture near candle. Let candle burn completely out. Take wax and paper and form a ball. Anoint wax ball with both oils again saying the verses of Psalm. Hide wax ball until person released then destroy it. So mote it be.

Psalm 142 v 1-2-6-7

1   *I cried unto the LORD with my voice; with my voice unto the LORD did I make my supplication.*

2   *I poured out my complaint before him; I showed before him my trouble.*

6   *Attend unto my cry; for I am brought very low: deliver me from my persecutors; for they are stronger than I.*

7   *Bring my soul out of prison, that I may praise thy name: the righteous shall compass me about; for thou shalt deal bountifully with me.*

~~~~~~~~~~ *** ~~~~~~~~~~

Psalm 142 - Protection from the law
Very powerful working to keep you safe and unseen by law enforcement.

Day: All
Herb: Fennel Seed-2 teaspoons, Snake Root-1 piece, Rue

powder-2 teaspoons
Candle: 7 Day-Law Stay Away
Oil: Law Stay Away
Other: small blue cotton/flannel bag, white string

Anoint candle, bag and self with oil while saying verses of Psalm aloud. Light the candle. Place all herbs in bag and secure with white string. Put bag beside candle and let stay there overnight. In the morning take bag and hold with both hands while saying verses of Psalm aloud. Keep the bag with you for as long as needed. Let no one touch it. Let candle completely burn out. So mote it be.

Psalm 142 v 4-5-6

4   *I looked on my right hand, and beheld, but there was no man that would know me: refuge failed me; no man cared for my soul.*

5   *I cried unto thee, O LORD: I said, Thou art my refuge and my portion in the land of the living.*

6   *Attend unto my cry; for I am brought very low: deliver me from my persecutors; for they are stronger than I.*

7

Prophecy-Influencing Others-Dreams

For prophecy never had its origin in the human will, but prophets, though human, spoke from God as they were carried along by the Holy Spirit. 2 Peter 1:21

He said, "Hear now My words: If there is a prophet among you, I, the LORD, shall make Myself known to him in a vision I shall speak with him in a dream. Numbers 12:6

Magickal Tidbit
Light a Divinity candle and say Lord's Prayer whenever feel evil is near.
Keep a copy of the Lord's Prayer in your wallet for protection.
Put a copy of Lord's Prayer in the wall of a newly built or renovated house for blessings.

~~~~~~~~~~ *** ~~~~~~~~~~

Psalm 49 - Gaining the second sight-prophecy
We all have the ability to become a prophet and be filled with the Holy Spirit. This working is inspired by a working of Marie Laveau used in the 1880's.

Day: All-After Sunset
Candle: White-7 day
Oil: Prophecy
Incense: Cinnamon powder-1 teaspoon, Voodoo Incense powder-4 tablespoon, Sandalwood Incense-4 tablespoon, Vertivert powder-2 tablespoon, Benzoin powder-1 teaspoon

This is a seven day working that when done correctly will give the vision of things to come. Blend all incense together. Place mixture in a sealed container in a cool dark place. On first evening, anoint candle with oil and light. Take approx. 1 tablespoon of incense mixture and burn. Read Psalm slowly and with strong convention. For next six days while candle burns, repeat each evening. Burn a little of incense mixture and recite the Psalm. So mote it be.

Psalm 49 v 1-4

1   *Hear this, all ye people; give ear, all ye inhabitants of the world:*

2   *Both low and high, rich and poor, together.*

3   *My mouth shall speak of wisdom; and the meditation of my heart shall be of understanding.*

4   *I will incline mine ear to a parable: I will open my dark saying upon the harp.*

~~~~~~~~~~ *** ~~~~~~~~~~

Psalm 78 - Increasing psychic abilities

We are all born with a sixth sense or third eye but we must develop and learn to use this ability. This working will aid you in that goal.

Day: All
Incense: Sandalwood-1/2 cup, Cinnamon-1 teaspoon, Wormwood-3 teaspoons, Solomon's Seal powder-1 teaspoon, Dragon's Blood powder-1/2 teaspoon, Saltpeter-pinch
Other: Parchment paper, Dragon's Blood ink, sea salt

Combine all incense ingredients together and store in an airtight container in cool, dry place. Mixture is good for 30 days (write date made on tape and put on bottom of container so can remember). Write the following lines on parchment paper using Dragon's Blood ink.--"That which is unknown to me will be known. That which is unseen to me will be seen. That which is unspoken to me will be spoken."

Make a small circle (approx. 2ft) using/sprinkling sea salt. Place parchment paper in center of circle. Burn 2 tablespoons of incense mixture in the west of the circle. Repeat three times the verses of the Psalm aloud. Take parchment and place in west with incense, put more incense on top of paper so burns completely to ash. As paper burns, again say verses aloud. So mote it be.

Psalm 78 v 1-4

1   *Give ear, O my people, to my law: incline your ears to the words of my mouth.*

2   *I will open my mouth in a parable: I will utter dark sayings of old:*

3   *Which we have heard and known, and our fathers have told us.*

4   *We will not hide them from their children, showing to the generation to come the praises of the LORD, and his strength, and his wonderful works that he hath done.*

~~~~~~~~~~ *** ~~~~~~~~~~

Psalm 114 - Influencing others with your thoughts

When you need others to see things your way that will influence a positive outcome for all involved. This is not a working to use for dark matters.

Day: All
Herb: Tonka beans-9, Vervain-2 teaspoons, Five Finger Grass-2 teaspoons
Oil: Compelling
Other: mason jar, piece of red cotton material large enough to cover top of jar, white chalk, red string/yarn

Anoint Tonka beans with compelling oil and place in jar. Read verses of Psalm then sit jar upon written copy of Psalms. Blend other herbs together and sprinkle over Tonka beans in jar. Put nine drops Compelling oil on top. Securely close jar with lid. Place red cotton material on top of jar and secure with red string/yarn. Using white chalk make the sign of the cross on the material. Then draw an "X" on top of cross. In center of lines crossing make a small circle. Place nine drops Compelling oil in center while saying aloud "Do as I say" nine times. Place jar in secret place, leave there until you get desired results, then destroy it. So mote it be.

Psalm 114

1   When Israel went out of Egypt, the house of Jacob from a people of strange language;

2   Judah was his sanctuary, and Israel his dominion.

3   The sea saw it, and fled: Jordan was driven back.

4   The mountains skipped like rams, and the little hills like lambs.

5   What ailed thee, O thou sea, that thou fleddest? thou Jordan, that thou was driven back?

6   Ye mountains, that ye skipped like rams; and ye little hills, like lambs?

7   Tremble, thou earth, at the presence of the Lord, at the presence of the God of Jacob;

8   Which turned the rock into a standing water, the flint into a fountain of waters.

~~~~~~~~~~ *** ~~~~~~~~~~

Psalm 64 - Stopping someone from telling your secrets

This protective working will stop people from being able to divulge/tell the secrets you told them. They will not be able to use your words against you.

Day: During the hours of Mars
Incense: Helping Hand
Other: Low John the Conqueror Root-1 piece

Once you start this working it is very important that you do not gossip or speak of this person in any negative way. You must show your worthiness in deeds, actions and words. For seven days rise each morning and read the Psalm aloud. Using the table below burn Helping Hand incense during the hours of Mars once daily for the seven days. At the end of the seven days take a small piece of the root and put on the front doorstep of the person you want to keep quiet. Keep rest of root on your person at all times. So mote it be.

Hours of Mars
Sunday- 2 pm, 4 pm, 9 pm, 11 pm
Monday- 6 am, 1 pm, 8 pm
Tuesday- 3 am, 10 am, 5 pm, 12 midnight
Wednesday- 7 am, 2 pm, 9 pm
Thursday- 4 am, 11 am, 6 pm
Friday- 1 am, 8 am, 3 pm, 11 pm
Saturday- 5 am, 12 noon, 7 pm

Psalm 64

1   *Hear my voice, O God, in my prayer: preserve my life from fear of the enemy.*
2   *Hide me from the secret counsel of the wicked; from the insurrection of the workers of iniquity:*
3   *Who whet their tongue like a sword, and bend their bows to shoot their arrows, even bitter words:*
4   *That they may shoot in secret at the perfect: suddenly do they shoot at him, and fear not.*
5   *They encourage themselves in an evil matter: they commune of laying snares privily; they say, Who shall see them?*

6   *They search out iniquities; they accomplish a diligent search: both the inward thought of every one of them, and the heart, is deep.*

7   *But God shall shoot at them with an arrow; suddenly shall they be wounded.*

8   *So they shall make their own tongue to fall upon themselves: all that see them shall flee away.*

9   *And all men shall fear, and shall declare the work of God; for they shall wisely consider of his doing.*

10 *The righteous shall be glad in the LORD, and shall trust in him; and all the upright in heart shall glory.*

~~~~~~~~~~ ******* ~~~~~~~~~~

Psalm 70 - Stopping someone from working against you

When you know someone is trying to bewitch you or bring foul energies around you, your family or house use this working to help keep safe all you hold dear.

Day: Full moon
Incense: Helping hand
Candles: Black & Red Double Action, 7 Day-White Protection
Other: Uncrossing powder, sea salt (pure, unrefined), 1 full sheet of parchment paper cut in half, dove's blood ink

This working is done in two parts. The first part needs to be done before midnight and the second part done after midnight. Take care and prepare yourself properly before starting (take a good cleansing bath/shower, cleanse/smudge space). Start the first part of your working by saying aloud Psalm 23 while making a small circle of salt. Light white candle and place in center of circle. On one piece of parchment using Dove's blood ink draw seven circles inside of each other. Start with a small circle and draw six more, each bigger around it. On other side of paper write your full name three times. Sprinkle uncrossing powder on the paper and place it under the white candle. Say aloud the verses of the Psalm below while concentrating on the flame of the candle. Leave candle to burn completely out. Next part should be started after midnight. Again start with saying the 23rd Psalm and making a small circle with salt. You can do this right beside the white candle circle but do not let the two circles touch. Light black & red double action candle and place in center of circle. Using the Dove's blood ink draw a large X on other half of parchment paper with small X's drawn in all four corners of the paper. Write your full name three times on the other side of paper. Sprinkle paper with uncrossing powder and put under black & red candle. Again say verses of Psalm below while concentrating on the flame of the candle. Leave candle to burn completely out. When both candles have gone out take parchment paper from both candles and burn. Do not speak of what you have done to anyone. So mote it be.

Psalm 70

1   *Make haste, o God, to deliver me; make haste to help me, O Lord.*

2   *Let them be ashamed and confounded that seek after my soul: let them be turned backward, and put to confusion, that desire my hurt.*

3   *Let them be turned back for a reward of their shame that say, Aha, aha.*

4   *Let all those that seek thee rejoice and be glad in thee: and let such as love thy salvation say continually, Let God be magnified.*

5   *But I am poor and needy: make haste unto me, O God: thou art my help and my deliverer; O Lord, make no tarrying.*

~~~~~~~~~~ *** ~~~~~~~~~~

Psalm 119 - Needing others to accomplish a goal

When you know what needs to be done and need the help of others to do this. Use this working to aid you in getting others to do as you need.

Day: All
Oil: High Conquering
Other: Lodestone-2

Anoint Lodestones with oil while reading verses of Psalm. Hold Lodestones in left hand and concentrate on the results/goal you want to have. Envision people willingly helping you achieve this. Keep Lodestones with you until get desired results. So mote it be.

Psalm 119 v 26-31

26 *I have declared my ways, and thou heardest me: teach me thy statutes.*

27 *Make me to understand the way of thy precepts: so shall I talk of thy wondrous works.*

28 *My soul melteth for heaviness: strengthen thou me according unto thy word.*

29 *Remove from me the way of lying: and grant me thy law graciously.*

30 *I have chosen the way of truth: thy judgments have I laid before me.*

31 *I have stuck unto thy testimonies: O LORD, put me not to shame.*

~~~~~~~~~~ *** ~~~~~~~~~~

Psalm 119 - Wanting people to agree with you

Are you dealing with a person who stubbornly won't see eye to eye with you? Do you need people to see things your way? This working will help you to achieve that goal.

Day: All
Herb: Dill Weed-pinch, Cascara Sagrada-pinch
Other: parchment paper

Place herbs on parchment and fold paper to secure mixture. Read verses of Psalm aloud while doing this. Carry packet in your pocket for three days. On the third day open paper and sprinkle mixture where you know the people will walk that you want to influence. So mote it be.

Psalm 119 v 41-45

41 *Let thy mercies come also unto me, O LORD, even thy salvation, according to thy word.*

42 *So shall I have wherewith to answer him that reproacheth me: for I trust in thy word.*

43 *And take not the word of truth utterly out of my mouth; for I have hoped in thy judgments.*

44 *So shall I keep thy law continually forever and ever.*

45 *And I will walk at liberty: for I seek thy precepts.*

~~~~~~~~~~ *** ~~~~~~~~~~

Psalm 130 - Seeking aid from others

Use this working for when needing people to help you in getting a goal done. Not good for financial matters.

Day: Thurs
Herb: Tonka Beans- 3
Oil: High Conquering
Other: Compelling powder, Lucky Blueing-1 bottle

For three days take a bath every day adding three drops of oil to water. Afterwards rub your ankles, wrist and chest with Compelling powder. When done say verses of Psalm aloud several times until the words start to blur together and you can feel the energy. Add seven drops of Lucky Blueing to your laundry for washing clothes. So mote it be.

Psalm 130 v 1-2-7-8

1   *Out of the depths have I cried unto thee, O LORD.*
2   *Lord, hear my voice: let thine ears be attentive to the voice of my supplications. 7 Let Israel hope in the LORD: for with the LORD there is mercy, and with him is plenteous redemption.*
8   *And he shall redeem Israel from all his iniquities.*

~~~~~~~~~~ *** ~~~~~~~~~~

Psalm 140 - Stopping violent actions of others

A little dark Magick is sometimes needed. When you know that a person is filled with evil and potentially dangerous use this working to stop them from harming you.

Day: Friday
Herb: Black Mustard seed-1 teaspoon
Oil: Divine Savior
Candles: Taper-White & Black
Other: 5 pieces of parchment paper-half paper size, picture of person, sea salt, 3 black chicken feathers, goofer's dust or graveyard dirt, small glass of water, glue stick, fireproof container, torch oil

This working needs to start right after midnight. Remember to properly prepare yourself and the space working in (directions are in the front of the book). Cut picture of person into five pieces. Glue each piece to half a sheet of parchment. Use glue stick to draw a large X across each sheet/picture. Sprinkle with graveyard dirt so sticks to glue. Let dry for at least 15 minutes. Anoint candles and self with oil. Place candles side by side about a foot apart. Between them place the glass of water and three feathers. Sprinkle mustard seed around both candles. Light the candles while saying verses of Psalm aloud (if is a woman replace word where needed). Stand in the East facing candles and toss small handful of salt over shoulder. Repeat at South, West, and North points. Next lay pieces of parchment around candles forming a small circle. Walking clockwise around circle nine times repeat the following- 'Black of heart you may be. The Divine protects me.' When done pick up each piece of paper while saying a verse of the Psalm, spit on it and place in fireproof container. There are 5 verses and five pieces of paper. Remember to say each verse with deep emotion and conviction. Pour small amount of torch oil in container on top of paper. Light it carefully. As papers burn again say verses of the Psalm aloud. Make sure all the paper is burned to ash. Use more torch oil if needed. Leave black and white candles to completely burn out. Next morning throw the ashes to the wind and pour out glass of water unto ground. Bury any candle wax left. So mote it be.

Psalm 140 v 1-2-4-6-10

1   Deliver me, O LORD, from the evil man: preserve me from the violent man;

2   Which imagine mischiefs in their heart; continually are they gathered together for war.

4   Keep me, O LORD, from the hands of the wicked; preserve me from the violent man; who have purposed to overthrow my goings.

6   I said unto the LORD, Thou art my God: hear the voice of my supplications, O LORD.

10 Let burning coals fall upon them: let them be cast into the fire; into deep pits that they rise not up again.

~~~~~~~~~~ *** ~~~~~~~~~~

Psalm 95 - Having dreams of things to come

Use this working with caution, you may see things that are not meant to be seen. Only are careful consideration should this working be used. Not to be done for trivial matters. Not a good working for beginner's.

Day: Dark Moon
Oil: Psychic
Other: Seal of Spiritual Assistance

Anoint self with oil. Sit quietly and read verses of Psalm several times. Place seal under your mattress at head of bed. Each night read Psalm until you have results. So mote it be.

Psalm 95

1   O come, let us sing unto the LORD: let us make a joyful noise to the rock of our salvation.

2   Let us come before his presence with thanksgiving, and make a joyful noise unto him with psalms.

3   For the LORD is a great God, and a great King above all gods.

4   In his hand are the deep places of the earth: the strength of the hills is his also.

5   The sea is his, and he made it: and his hands formed the dry land.

6   O come, let us worship and bow down: let us kneel before the LORD our maker.

7   For he is our God; and we are the people of his pasture, and the sheep of his hand. Today if ye will hear his voice,

8   Harden not your heart, as in the provocation, and as in the day of temptation in the wilderness:

9   When your fathers tempted me, proved me, and saw my work.

10   Forty years long was I grieved with this generation, and said, It is a people that do err in their heart, and they have not known my ways:

11   *Unto whom I swore in my wrath that they should not enter into my rest.*

~~~~~~~~~~ *** ~~~~~~~~~~

Psalm 112 - Dreaming of what the future can be

Do you want the possibilities of your life revealed to you? Are you ready to see all of your potential? Let this working help you to follow your dreams. All things are possible in the Light of Divinity.

Day: All
Incense: Sandalwood-1/2 cup, Musk powder-1/2 cup, Voodoo Incense powder-1/2 cup, Solomon's Seal powder-2 teaspoons, Aloes powder-1/2 teaspoon, Dragon's Blood powder-1/2 teaspoon, Saltpeter-1/2 teaspoon

Blend all ingredients together and store in an airtight container. Each evening right before going to bed read the verses of Psalm and burn a little of the incense mixture. Do this every night until you dream of what you need/want to know. So mote it be.

Psalm 112 v 1-2-3-4-5-9

1   *Praise ye the LORD. Blessed is the man that feareth the LORD, that delighteth greatly in his commandments.*

2   *His seed shall be mighty upon earth: the generation of the upright shall be blessed.*

3   *Wealth and riches shall be in his house: and his righteousness endureth forever. 4 Unto the upright there ariseth light in the darkness: he is gracious, and full of compassion, and righteous.*

5   *A good man showeth favour, and lendeth: he will guide his affairs with discretion.*

9   *He hath dispersed, he hath given to the poor; his righteousness endureth forever; his horn shall be exalted with honour.*

8

Self-Family-Children

For we are God's masterpiece. He has created us anew in Christ Jesus,
so we can do the good things he planned for us long ago.
Ephesian 2:10

Your descendants will be like the dust of the earth, and you will
spread out to the west and to the east, to the north and to the south.
All peoples on earth will be blessed through you and your offspring.
Genesis 28:14

Magickal Tidbit
Keep a little pile of money in center of home to attract more.
Never count your money in front of strangers, could cause your
luck to leave.
Placing a purse on the floor may jinx your money.

~~~~~~~~~~ ***** ~~~~~~~~~~

Psalm 115 - Being popular
Do you want everyone to know your name? Is the spotlight your
dream? Then this working is just the thing to aid you in making
all that happen.

Day: All
Oil: Attraction
Herbal Bath: Blue Vervain-2 teaspoons, Marigold powder-
1teaspoon, Lemon Verbena-1 teaspoon, Calamus powder-1
teaspoon, Quince seed (crushed)-1 teaspoon

Blend all herbal bath ingredients and let seep in a ½ gallon of spring water for three days. Strain out herbs and use ¼ cup of the water in your bath daily. Add three drops Attraction oil to your bath also. Each night before going to bed read the verses of the Psalm aloud several times. Do this working for nine days straight to guarantee success. So mote it be.

Psalm 115 v 11-15

11   *Ye that fear the LORD, trust in the LORD: he is their help and their shield.*

12   *The LORD hath been mindful of us: he will bless us; he will bless the house of Israel; he will bless the house of Aaron.*

13   *He will bless them that fear the LORD, both small and great.*

14   *The LORD shall increase you more and more, you and your children.*

15   *Ye are blessed of the LORD which made heaven and earth.*

~~~~~~~~~~ *** ~~~~~~~~~~

Psalm 19 - Acting/Speaking wisely

When you are looking to speak wise words and act in a positive way this will help you. Also stops dark and dangerous thoughts, helping to keep you in the Light of Divinity.

Day: All
Incense: Helping Hands
Herb: Sage bundle
Candle: 7 Day-White Spiritual
Oil: Peace oil

This is a 21 day working and requires 3-4 candles to burn for entire time. As soon as you realize one candle has gone out light a new one. If for some reason all 3 burns out before 21 days go get another candle to finish time remaining.

Smudge all rooms of house with sage bundle while saying

Psalms 23. Light the candle and recite the followings verses three times. Let candle burn completely out. When lighting next candle again recite verses three times. Do again for next candle for a total of 21 days. You should feel a difference within three days of lighting first candle. So mote it be.

Psalm 19 v 7-8-14

7   *The law of the LORD is perfect, converting the soul: the testimony of the LORD is sure, making wise the simple.*

8   *The statutes of the LORD are right, rejoicing the heart: the commandment of the LORD is pure, enlightening the eyes.*

14 *Let the words of my mouth, and the meditation of my heart, be acceptable in thy sight, O LORD, my strength, and my redeemer.*

~~~~~~~~~~ ***** ~~~~~~~~~~

Psalm 24 - Keeping oneself from acting in revenge

When wanting help with taking the higher road in a situation. This is "putting it in God's hands" and letting God's just judgement guide you.

Day: Any
Candle: Taper-White or Green
Other: parchment paper
Herbal Bath: 2 tablespoons-Lovage, 4 tablespoons-Jasmine, 2 tablespoons- crushed Tonka Beans

Blend all the herbs together and place in a small white cotton bag. Tie bag tightly shut with a red string or thread. Draw a hot bath and place bag in it. Wait 15 minutes then enjoy a leisurely bath. Afterwards place bag in airtight container and re-use (approx. 3-4 baths). Then sit in your quiet place and recite verses seven times, light the candle. Write on paper "May the evening star light my way, God is within me". Let candle burn until you feel ready-pinch out. Fold paper in half and bury in place you walk every day. If can't do that, bury in houseplant in your house. You want to put this energy to the earth in some way. Be creative if necessary; jar of dirt. Repeat this herbal bath as many times as necessary until feel at peace. So mote it be.

Psalm 24 v 3-4-5

3   *Who shall ascend into the hill of the LORD? Or who shall stand in his holy place?*

4   *He that hath clean hands, and a pure heart; who hath not lifted up his soul unto vanity, nor sworn deceitfully.*

5   *He shall receive the blessing from the LORD, and righteousness from the God of his salvation.*

~~~~~~~~~~ *** ~~~~~~~~~~

Psalm 25 - Finding inner strength/overcoming addictions

When needing strength in facing difficult truths. Give your addiction to God and let Him guide you through this.

Day: All
Incense: Frankincense-1/3 cup, Myrhh-1/4 cup, Sandalwood-1/4 cup, Sacred Bark- ½ cup
Candle: Taper-Red
Other: Parchment paper, charcoal

This is a 3 day working and should start at sunrise on first day. Blend all incense together and burn on a piece of charcoal. Sit quietly and think about all the blessings you have: family, friends, safe place, reliable car, etc. When feel ready write all the blessings you have on one side of the paper. Fold paper three times, place under candle and light the candle. Read the verses three times.

Let candle burn until you feel ready then pinch out. Next two mornings read the blessings you wrote on parchment and put back under candle, light the candle and read verses three times. Again let candle burn until you feel ready to pinch out. On the third day after reading the verses write what you desire to overcome on back of paper. Light paper with candle and let burn to ash. Pinch out candle when done. Candle can be re-used. So mote it be.

Psalm 25 v 1-7

1   *Unto thee, O LORD, do I lift up my soul.*

2   *O my God, I trust in thee: let me not be ashamed, let not mine enemies triumph over me.*

3   *Yea, let none that wait on thee be ashamed: let them be ashamed which transgress without cause.*

4   *Show me thy ways, O LORD; teach me thy paths.*

5   *Lead me in thy truth, and teach me: for thou art the God of my salvation; on thee do I wait all the day.*

6   *Remember, O LORD, thy tender mercies and thy loving kindnesses; for they have been ever of old.*

7   *Remember not the sins of my youth, nor my transgressions: according to thy mercy remember thou me for thy goodness' sake, O LORD.*

~~~~~~~~~~ *** ~~~~~~~~~~

Psalm 106 - Being attractive/self

Let the beauty that is within you shine on the outside for all to see. Make yourself appear younger and more desirable with this working.

Day: All
Candles: Taper-7 Pink
Oil: Special No. 20, Van Van Perfume Oil
Other: Come To Me Powder

This is a 15 day working that once started you must continue to the end or start over. Each day- Use three drops Van Van Perfume Oil in your bath, sprinkle Come to Me Powder on neck and chest area, and put three drops Special No. 20 oil on the clothes you are going to wear. On the 15th day line up pink candles and light starting from left to right. Sit in front of candles and visualize yourself being attractive, desirable and/or younger. Read verses of Psalm aloud several times. Let candles burn for approx. 15 minutes and then pinch out. Candles can be reused. So mote it be.

Psalm 106 v 3-4-5

3 Blessed are they that keep judgment, and he that doeth righteousness at all times.

4 Remember me, O LORD, with the favour that thou bearest unto thy people: O visit me with thy salvation;

5 That I may see the good of thy chosen, that I may rejoice in the gladness of thy nation, that I may glory with thine inheritance.

~~~~~~~~~~ *** ~~~~~~~~~~

Psalm 117 - Failing through forgetfulness or carelessness

The roots of this working dates to the time of the Israelis. Seems we still have some of the same problems they had. When you know it is your fault and the intent was not negative or harmful this working will help to bring things back to right.

Day: Tuesday or New Moon
Incense: Helping Hand, John the Conqueror
Candle: Taper-Red
Oil: Protection, Jinx Removing
Other: Sea salt
Burn incense. Make approx. a 4 ft. circle (large enough for candle and you to kneel in) using sea salt. Anoint candle and

self with both oils. Place candle on North edge of circle. Kneel in middle towards candle. Light the candle and say verses of Psalm aloud ending each verse with-'My spirit is God's spirit. All will be forgiven.' Repeat several times until feel satisfied. When done pinch out candle and sweep salt away. So mote it be.

Psalm 117

1   *O praise the LORD, all ye nations: praise him, all ye people.*
2   *For his merciful kindness is great toward us: and the truth of the LORD endureth forever. Praise ye the LORD.*

~~~~~~~~~~ *** ~~~~~~~~~~

Psalm 119 - Helping to keep your promise

Having problems keeping a promise you made? Use this working to aid you in finding a way to make sure that your word is your bond. Success will be yours and what you promised will be done.

Day: All
Candle: 7 Day-Trinity
Oil: Success

Anoint candle with oil and light. Anoint self with oil and say verses of Psalm aloud. Each day the candle burns anoint self and read verses. So mote it be.

Psalm 119 v 1-8

1   *Blessed are the undefiled in the way, who walk in the law of the LORD.*
2   *Blessed are they that keep his testimonies, and that seek him with the whole heart.*
3   *They also do no iniquity: they walk in his ways.*
4   *Thou hast commanded us to keep thy precepts diligently.*

5   *O that my ways were directed to keep thy statutes!*

6   *Then shall I not be ashamed, when I have respect unto all thy commandments.*

7   *I will praise thee with uprightness of heart, when I shall have learned thy righteous judgments.*

8   *I will keep thy statutes: O forsake me not utterly.*

~~~~~~~~~~ *** ~~~~~~~~~~

Psalm 119 - Loneliness

Are you seeking the company of family and friends? Does no one seem to be stopping by your place? Use this working to attract the company of others.

Day: All at Midnight
Herb: Four Leaf Clover powder, Rosemary powder/crushed-equal amounts

Sprinkle herbal mixture across all doorways while reading verses of Psalm aloud. Soon your house will be full of family and friends. So mote it be.

Psalm 119 v57-64

57   *Thou art my portion, O LORD: I have said that I would keep thy words.*

58   *I intreated thy favour with my whole heart: be merciful unto me according to thy word.*

59   *I thought on my ways, and turned my feet unto thy testimonies.*

60   *I made haste, and delayed not to keep thy commandments.*

61   *The bands of the wicked have robbed me: but I have not forgotten thy law.*

62   *At midnight I will rise to give thanks unto thee because of thy righteous judgments.*

63   *I am a companion of all them that fear thee, and of them that*

keep thy precepts. 64 The earth, O LORD, is full of thy mercy: teach me thy statutes.

~~~~~~~~~~ *** ~~~~~~~~~~

Psalm 101 - Letting go of bad habits

Wanting to make a change in yourself for the better? Use this working to aid you in that journey.

Day: Sunday
Incense: Frankincense-4 tablespoons, Myrrh-3 tablespoons, Sandalwood-3 tablespoons, Saltpeter-1/2 teaspoon, Sacred Bark(crushed)-1/2 cup, Mandrake Root(crushed)-1 teaspoon, Saffron powder-2 teaspoons
Candle: 7 Day-Black
Oil: Success

This seven day working should start on Sunday morning first light of day. Mix all incense ingredients together and store in airtight container in cool dark place. Anoint black candle with oil. When ready burn small amount of incense and light the candle. Say verses of Psalm three times aloud then say what it is you want to change/leave/stop. Repeat for next six days. Be patience with results, this is a slow building working and it will take time. Results for some may take a little while. So mote it be.

Psalm 101 v1-4

1   *I will sing of mercy and judgment: unto thee, O LORD, will I sing.*

2   *I will behave myself wisely in a perfect way. O when wilt thou come unto me? I will walk within my house with a perfect heart.*

3   *I will set no wicked thing before mine eyes: I hate the work of them that turn aside; it shall not cleave to me.*

4   *A forward heart shall depart from me: I will not know a*

wicked person.

~~~~~~~~~~ *** ~~~~~~~~~~

Psalm 119 - Helping stop bad habits

When you need help in stopping or changing habits that are negative or hurtful.

Day: New Moon
Herbal Bath: Poke root-2 teaspoons, Five Finger Grass-4 teaspoons, Lavender-1/2 cup Oil: Success

Seep herbs in a gallon of spring water for three days. Drain herbs and use ¼ cup of water in your bath daily for seven days. Each day upon rising read the verses of the Psalm aloud. So mote it be.

Psalm 119 v33-40

33 *Teach me, O LORD, the way of thy statutes; and I shall keep it unto the end. 34 Give me understanding, and I shall keep thy law; yea, I shall observe it with my whole heart.*

35 *Make me to go in the path of thy commandments; for therein do I delight.*

36 *Incline my heart unto thy testimonies, and not to covetousness.*

37 *Turn away mine eyes from beholding vanity; and quicken thou me in thy way.*

38 *Stablish thy word unto thy servant, who is devoted to thy fear.*

39 *Turn away my reproach which I fear: for thy judgments are good.*

40 *Behold, I have longed after thy precepts: quicken me in thy righteousness.*

~~~~~~~~~~ *** ~~~~~~~~~~

Psalm 119 - Letting go of the past

When the memories of the past fill your days use this working to cleanse yourself and look forward to the future. Look to tomorrow with wonderment and joy. Stay in the Light of Divinity and you will find peace.

Day: All
Herbal Bath: Lovage, Juniper Berries (crushed), Tonka Beans (powdered)-1 teaspoon each, Jasmine, Rosemary-2 teaspoons each
Oil: Peace

Place herbs in small cotton bag. Seep bag in bath water for several minutes. Remove bag and place in airtight container to be used again. Can be used up to ten times. Also add six drops of Peace oil to bathwater. Afterwards sit quietly and read verses of Psalm. Do daily until feel better. So mote it be.

Psalm 119 v 65-72

65 *Thou hast dealt well with thy servant, O LORD, according unto thy word.*

66 *Teach me good judgment and knowledge: for I have believed thy commandments.*

67 *Before I was afflicted I went astray: but now have I kept thy word.*

68 *Thou art good, and doest good; teach me thy statutes.*

69 *The proud have forged a lie against me: but I will keep thy precepts with my whole heart.*

70 *Their heart is as fat as grease; but I delight in thy law.*

71 *It is good for me that I have been afflicted; that I might learn thy statutes.*

72 *The law of thy mouth is better unto me than thousands of gold and silver.*

~~~~~~~~~~ ***** ~~~~~~~~~~

Psalm 119 - Helping stop worry

When you can't stop thinking/worrying about a situation or matter use this working to help you to clear your mind.

Day: All
Incense: Helping Hand, John the Conqueror
Candle: 7 Day-White/ Peace
Oil: Peace
Other: Glass of spring water

Anoint candle with peace oil while saying verses of Psalm aloud. Light both incense, equal amounts/sticks. Light the candle and place glass of water in front of candle. Sit in front of candle and say the verses seven times aloud. Next morning pour out glass of water. Leave candle to burn out completely. Repeat if feel necessary. So mote it be.

Psalm 119 v 142-144

142 *Thy righteousness is an everlasting righteousness, and thy law is the truth. 143 Trouble and anguish have taken hold on me: yet thy commandments are my delights.*

144 *The righteousness of thy testimonies is everlasting: give me understanding, and I shall live.*

~~~~~~~~~~ ***** ~~~~~~~~~~

Psalm 129 - Having a successful life

This is a very popular charm can be found in use today along the SC/GA coastlines.

Day: All
Herb: Red clover-dried-2 teaspoons

Oil: Success

Other: Lodestone-1piece, red cotton bag

Before starting this working make sure to cleanse and bless Lodestone (use working for blessing a talisman, Psalm 86). Anoint self, bag and Lodestone with oil. Place Lodestone and Red clover in bag. Tie or sew bag shut. Hold bag in both hands and repeat entire Psalm nine times aloud. Keep bag with you at all times. Let no one touch it. So mote it be.

Psalm 129

1   Many a time have they afflicted me from my youth, may Israel now say:

2   Many a time have they afflicted me from my youth: yet they have not prevailed against me.

3   The plowers plowed upon my back: they made long their furrows.

4   The LORD is righteous: he hath cut asunder the cords of the wicked.

5   Let them all be confounded and turned back that hate Zion.

6   Let them be as the grass upon the housetops, which withereth afore it groweth up:

7   Wherewith the mower filleth not his hand; nor he that bindeth sheaves his bosom.

8   Neither do they which go by say, The blessing of the LORD be upon you: we bless you in the name of the LORD.

~~~~~~~~~~ *** ~~~~~~~~~~

Psalm 97 - Uniting a quarreling family

Are family gatherings full of strive and arguments in your house? Do you just want everyone to get along? This working will help to create peaceful energies around everyone.

Day: All
Herb: Rosemary, Sage, Dill, Thyme (fresh if possible, dried if you must)

This is a wonderful kitchen/cooking working. Fix a favorite dish adding the herbs listed. Each time you add a different herb to the dish say verses of Psalm aloud. So mote it be.

Psalm 97 v 9-12

9   *For thou, LORD, art high above all the earth: thou art exalted far above all gods.*

10 *Ye that love the LORD, hate evil: he preserveth the souls of his saints; he delivereth them out of the hand of the wicked.*

11 *Light is sown for the righteous, and gladness for the upright in heart.*

12 *Rejoice in the LORD, ye righteous; and give thanks at the remembrance of his holiness.*

~~~~~~~~~~ *** ~~~~~~~~~~

Psalm 98 - Bringing peace to families

When the past needs to be let go of and the future looked forward to, this working will help the family to achieve that.

Day: All
Herb: Five finger grass, High John powder
Candles: Taper-7 Pink
Oil: Peace

Mix Five finger grass and High John powder together. Write the names of those you wish to get along on candles and anoint with Peace oil. Using herb mixture make a small circle and place the seven pink candles in it. Light the candles and say verses of Psalm. Let candles burn completely out. When done sweep up herbal mixture and sprinkle across doorway the people will walk through. So mote it be.

Psalm 98 v 6-9

6   *With trumpets and sound of cornet make a joyful noise before the LORD, the King.*
7   *Let the sea roar, and the fullness thereof; the world, and they that dwell therein.*
8   *Let the floods clap their hands: let the hills be joyful together*
9   *Before the LORD; for he cometh to judge the earth: with righteousness shall he judge the world, and the people with equity.*

~~~~~~~~~~ *** ~~~~~~~~~~

Psalm 133 - Creating harmony in your family

Think of this as a preemptive strike-before things can go wrong use this working to insure that they don't. Very good to use when have family gatherings or celebrating holidays together.

Day: All
Herb: fresh Rosemary, Thyme, Cloves
Candle: Taper-White
Oil: Harmony
Other: bowl/dish of white rice, glass of spring water

The day before the family gets together prepare rice and place on a pretty dish. Take dish and glass of spring water and place outside in quiet area. If can't do this put in a window facing west. Anoint candle with oil and light. Sprinkle oil across doorway people will use while saying verses aloud. Place small dishes of cloves in the rooms people will be in. Use fresh rosemary and thyme in food serving people. So mote it be.

Psalm 133

1   *Behold, how good and how pleasant it is for brethren to dwell together in unity!*

2   *It is like the precious ointment upon the head, that ran down upon the beard, even Aaron's beard: that went down to the skirts of his garments;*

3   *As the dew of Hermon, and as the dew that descended upon the mountains of Zion: for there the LORD commanded the blessing, even life for evermore.*

~~~~~~~~~~ *** ~~~~~~~~~~

Psalm 44 - Protecting children from harm

This very powerful working will help to insure that your child/ren are safe when you cannot be there.

Day: Full Moon
Candle: Taper-White
Herb: Woodruff & Mugwort
Oil: Protection
Other: Plant Mars Talisman/ Seal, full sheet parchment paper, red thread/yarn, a few strands of child/ren's hair (hint-get from hairbrush)

Rub candle with oil while saying the 23rd Psalm. On paper draw a large cross with finger using protection oil. Write child/ren's name on all four corners of paper in ink. Place talisman and hair in center of paper and fold corners to center. Bind securely with red thread. Light the candle and say verses while holding bound paper talisman close to your heart. When finished let candle burn for a time then pinch out. Place bundle under child's mattress at foot of bed. Sprinkle equal amounts of woodruff and mugwort in dresser drawers and closets used to store child's clothes. So mote it be.

Psalm 44 v 5-8

5   *Through thee will we push down our enemies: through thy*
    name will we tread them under that rise up against us.

6   *For I will not trust in my bow, neither shall my sword save me.*

7   *But thou hast saved us from our enemies, and hast put them to*
    shame that hated us.

8   *In God we boast all the day long, and praise thy name for ever.*
    Selah.

~~~~~~~~~~ ******* ~~~~~~~~~~

Psalm 45 - Wanting a child

Let God know that you desire a child above all else. Ask all the
Powers of Divinity for help in achieving this goal. This is a good
working when seeking adoption or other means of getting a child.
Use Psalm 102 if wanting to get pregnant.

Day: Tuesday or New Moon
Incense: Aloe & Musk
Herb: Basil and several fresh Rosemary twigs
Candle: Taper- Red
Oil: Lavender
Other: White thread

Burn incense. Wrap twigs of Rosemary together with white
thread while repeating the following seven times: "My spirit is
ready, my heart is ready, I am ready".

Rub candle with lavender oil. Place rosemary twigs beside the
candle then sit quietly and say the verses slowly. Light the candle
and envision yourself holding a child. While doing this place
lavender oil on your temples and inside of wrists. When you feel
ready pinch out candle then put the rosemary twigs under the
mattress at the foot of your bed. Use Basil in all your meals until
get a child. So mote it be.

Psalm 45 v 6-17

6   *Thy throne, O God, is for ever and ever: the sceptre of thy kingdom is a right sceptre.*

7   *Thou lovest righteousness, and hatest wickedness: therefore God, thy God, hath anointed thee with the oil of gladness above thy fellows.*

8   *All thy garments smell of myrrh, and aloes, and cassia, out of the ivory palaces, whereby they have made thee glad.*

9   *Kings' daughters were among thy honourable women: upon thy right hand did stand the queen in gold of Ophir.*

10   *Hearken, O daughter, and consider, and incline thine ear; forget also thine own people, and thy father's house;*

11   *So shall the king greatly desire thy beauty: for he is thy Lord; and worship thou him.*

12   *And the daughter of Tyre shall be there with a gift; even the rich among the people shall intreat thy favour.*

13   *The king's daughter is all glorious within: her clothing is of wrought gold.*

14   *She shall be brought unto the king in raiment of needlework: the virgins her companions that follow her shall be brought unto thee.*

15   *With gladness and rejoicing shall they be brought: they shall enter into the king's palace.*

16   *Instead of thy fathers shall be thy children, whom thou mayest make princes in all the earth.*

17   *I will make thy name to be remembered in all generations: therefore shall the people praise thee for ever and ever.*

~~~~~~~~~~ *** ~~~~~~~~~~

Psalm 102 - Becoming pregnant

When you know it is the right time to become a pregnant use this working to help move things along. Do not use if trying to entrap a man, for this working could turn into a curse of being barren forever. Gullah folk inspired this working and swear by the use of cinnamon for fertility.

Day: Wednesday
Herb: Basil (fresh), Cinnamon sticks-24
Candle: 7 Day-Yellow or The Cross of Caravaca
Oil: Cinnamon, Yang Ylang

This seven day working must be done from start to finish to get results.

Day 1- take long hot soak bath using the 12 sticks of cinnamon and six drops of cinnamon oil. Afterwards anoint candle with the Yang Ylang oil and light. Read verses of Psalm aloud.

Day 2- this day you must spend the day saying as many times as possible verse 28 of the Psalm.

Day 3- mix three drops Yang Ylang and Cinnamon oil together. Anoint self with mixture-dab on forehead, wrists, behind knees, bottoms of feet. Read verses of Psalm aloud.

Day 4-same as day 3

Day 5- same as day 3

Day 6-again take hot bath using 12 sticks cinnamon and six drops cinnamon oil.

Day 7- spend the day saying as many times as you can verse 28 until the sun sets.

Use fresh basil herb and cinnamon in your food every day until pregnant. So mote it be.

Psalm 102 v 16-17-18-28

16 *When the LORD shall build up Zion, he shall appear in his glory.*

17 *He will regard the prayer of the destitute, and not despise their prayer.*

18 *This shall be written for the generation to come: and the people which shall be created shall praise the LORD.*

28   *The children of thy servants shall continue, and their seed shall*
      be established before thee.

~~~~~~~~~~ *** ~~~~~~~~~~

Psalm 126 - Easing sorrow from a miscarriage

There is hope and possibilities even in the darkest times. Use this
working to give you strength and peace of mind.

Day: All
Herbal Tea: Hyssop blend
Candle: 7 Day-White Divinity
Other: 1 piece of Beth root

Light the candle. Place Beth root under foot of your bed. Sit
quietly and drink tea while repeating verses of Psalm several
times. Do this daily for as long as candle burns or until feel your
pain ease. So mote it be.

Psalm 126 v 3-5-6

3   *The LORD hath done great things for us; whereof we are glad.*
5   *They that sow in tears shall reap in joy.*
6   *He that goeth forth and weepeth, bearing precious seed, shall*
     doubtless come again with rejoicing, bringing his sheaves with
     him.

9

God-Forgiveness-Wisdom

Whoever conceals their sins does not prosper, but the one who confesses and renounces them finds mercy. Proverbs 28:13

Let the message of Christ dwell among you richly as you teach and admonish one another with all wisdom through psalms, hymns, and songs from the Spirit, singing to God with gratitude in your hearts. Colossians 3:16

Magickal Tidbit
Stir a pot clockwise to put good energies into the food. Parsley, sage and thyme fresh herbs should be added to family meals to promote peace and togetherness. Never cook when angry, make cause a sickness.

~~~~~~~~~~ *** ~~~~~~~~~~

Psalm 23 - Finding peace/staying in the Light of Divinity
The most well-known and powerful of the Psalms has been used since it was first said in helping to keep us in the Light of Divinity where no harm will come. Use this Psalm regularly and whenever feel the need.

Day: All
Incense: Blessing
Candle: Taper-White
Other: Parchment paper

Light the candle and burn incense. Recite this entire Psalms.

Write it on parchment and keep in wallet. Very good to recite whenever feel evil is near. So mote it be.

Psalm 23 v all

1   *The LORD is my shepherd; I shall not want.*

2   *He maketh me to lie down in green pastures: he leadeth me beside the still waters.*

3   *He restoreth my soul: he leadeth me in the paths of righteousness for his name's sake.*

4   *Yea, though I walk through the valley of the shadow of death, I will fear no evil: for thou art with me; thy rod and thy staff they comfort me*

5   *Thou prepares a table before me in the presence of mine enemies: thou anointest my head with oil; my cup runneth over.*

6   *Surely goodness and mercy shall follow me all the days of my life: and I will dwell in the house of the LORD forever.*

~~~~~~~~~~ *** ~~~~~~~~~~

Psalm 82 - Being pushed away from God

Do you feel as if someone is working against you to make you doubt the light of Divinity and draw you towards darkness? Are foul and hurtful words coming from your mouth but you don't know why you said it? Use this working to bring yourself closer to God and drive the darkness away.

Day: All
Oil: Holy
Incense: Patchouli powder-1/2 cup, Sage powder-2 tablespoons, Orris root powder-2 tablespoons, Wormwood powder-1 tablespoon
Herb: Queen Elizabeth root-1 piece
Candle: 7 Day- White Spiritual

Combine incense ingredients and store in airtight container. Light the candle. Burn incense. Say aloud the verses while anointing Queen Elizabeth root with Holy oil. Place root under the mattress of your bed. Burn incense mixture daily for as long as candle burns. So mote it be.

Psalm 82 v 1-6

1 God standeth in the congregation of the mighty; he judgeth among the gods.
2 How long will ye judge unjustly, and accept the persons of the wicked? Selah.
3 Defend the poor and fatherless: do justice to the afflicted and needy.
4 Deliver the poor and needy: rid them out of the hand of the wicked.
5 They know not, neither will they understand; they walk on in darkness: all the foundations of the earth are out of course.
6 I have said, Ye are gods; and all of you are children of the most High.

~~~~~~~~~~ *** ~~~~~~~~~~

Psalm 119 - Stopping doubts of faith

When you find yourself questioning Divinity and feeling like you are in a negative space use this working to bring balance and faith back onto your life. Also helps to set yourself up to receive life's blessings.

Day: Tuesday
Herbal Incense: Orris Root powder-1 teaspoon, Wood Bettany-3 teaspoons, Lotus powder-1/2 teaspoon, Saltpeter-pinch
Candle: 7 Day-Spiritual/White
Oil: Divine Savior

Other: Lodestone

This is a seven day working that must be completed from start to finish to see results. Blend all herbal ingredients together and store in an airtight container. Anoint candle with oil and light. Burn a small amount of incense. Anoint lodestone with oil and place beside candle. Say verses of Psalm aloud. Repeat each morning for as long as candle burns. When finished keep lodestone with you at all times and let no one touch it. So mote it be.

Psalm 119 v145-152

145 *I cried with my whole heart; hear me, O LORD: I will keep thy statutes.*

146 *I cried unto thee; save me, and I shall keep thy testimonies.*

147 *I prevented the dawning of the morning, and cried: I hoped in thy word.*

148 *Mine eyes prevent the night watches, that I might meditate in thy word.*

149 *Hear my voice according unto thy loving kindness: O LORD, quicken me according to thy judgment.*

150 *They draw nigh that follow after mischief: they are far from thy law.*

151 *Thou art near, O LORD; and all thy commandments are truth.*

152 *Concerning thy testimonies, I have known of old that thou hast founded them forever.*

~~~~~~~~~~ ******* ~~~~~~~~~~

Psalm 139 - Seeking to walk in Jesus' footsteps/spiritual calling

God is calling. Will you answer? Use this working to affirm the calling of faith. Consider this path wisely and with counsel, for its sacrifices are also its rewards.

Day: All
Incense: Nutmeg powder-1 teaspoon, Frankincense-1 teaspoon, Orris Root powder-1 teaspoon, Saltpeter-pinch
Candle: 7 Day-White/Divinity

Blend incense ingredients together and store in an airtight container. Light the candle and burn small amount of incense mixture. Read verses of Psalm aloud. Each day for as long as candle burns read verses and burn small amount of incense mixture. So mote it be.

Psalm 139 v 1-2-14-15-23-24

1 *O LORD, thou hast searched me, and known me.*
2 *Thou knowest my downsitting and mine uprising, thou understandest my thought afar off.*
14 *I will praise thee; for I am fearfully and wonderfully made: marvellous are thy works; and that my soul knoweth right well.*
15 *My substance was not hid from thee, when I was made in secret, and curiously wrought in the lowest parts of the earth.*
23 *Search me, O God, and know my heart: try me, and know my thoughts:*
24 *And see if there be any wicked way in me, and lead me in the way everlasting.*

~~~~~~~~~~ *** ~~~~~~~~~~

Psalm 150 - Affirming faith

Sometimes we need to be reminded that Divinity is not only solemn but also full of joy and laughter. Use this working to fill you with the wonderment and happiness that only Divinity can give you.

Day: All
Candle: 7 Day-White/Divinity

This Psalm is a true song and should be said in a song like voice that is loud and filled with joy. Light Divinity candle and each day it burns say the Psalm aloud. Let the words resonate inside you. So mote it be.

Psalm 150 v all

1   *Praise ye the LORD. Praise God in his sanctuary: praise him in the firmament of his power.*

2   *Praise him for his mighty acts: praise him according to his excellent greatness.*

3   *Praise him with the sound of the trumpet: praise him with the psaltery and harp.*

4   *Praise him with the timbrel and dance: praise him with stringed instruments and organs.*

5   *Praise him upon the loud cymbals: praise him upon the high sounding cymbals. 6 Let everything that hath breath praise the LORD. Praise ye the LORD.*

~~~~~~~~~~ *** ~~~~~~~~~~

Psalm 25 - Forgiving yourself

Sometimes this is the hardest thing we can do- to forgive ourselves. God has told us He will take our sins for us. Now you must let Him.

Day: All
Incense: Frankincense & Nutmeg
Herb: Mustard Seeds-9
Candle: Taper-Yellow
Oil: Blessings
Other: small dish or seashell

Burn incense, light the candle then sit quietly repeating the verses until feel a sense of calmness come over you. Place nine mustard seeds in a small dish/seashell with each one saying "I give unto My Lord my sin". Place dish/seashell in your garden or find a quiet place in the woods and put beside a large tree. So mote it be.

Psalm 25 v 11 & 20

11 *For thy name's sake, O LORD, pardon mine iniquity; for it is great.*

20 *O keep my soul, and deliver me: let me not be ashamed; for I put my trust in thee.*

~~~~~~~~~~ *** ~~~~~~~~~~

Psalm 32 - Seeking forgiveness of others

Sometimes we all need to be forgiven. This working will remind others that we are all not perfect and to find forgiveness in their heart.

Day: New Moon
Incense: John the Conqueror, Helping Hand –equal amounts
Candle: 7 Day-White

Burn incense. Light the candle and say verse. Then for as long as candle stays lit each morning say this verse. So mote it be.

Psalm 32 v 5

I acknowledged my sin unto thee, and mine iniquity have I not hid. I said, I will confess my transgressions unto the LORD; and thou forgave the iniquity of my sin. Selah.

~~~~~~~~~~ *** ~~~~~~~~~~

Psalm 51 - Seeking forgiveness for one's actions

When the soul is heavy with regrets and past mistakes this

working will take that weight away and put you in the Light of Divinity.

Day: All
Candle: White taper
Oil: Divine Savior
Incense: John the Conqueror & Helping Hand (equal amounts)
Herb: Hyssop-1/4 cup or Herbal bath blend containing Hyssop

The best place to do this entire working is in the bathroom where you will be taking a long hot bath. Run a nice hot bath and put Hyssop in bath water. If loose herb place in cotton bag to seep through. Anoint candle with oil and light. Burn the incense. Before getting in water read the verses of the Psalm slowly and with deep intent. Take your bath making sure to thoroughly cleanse yourself. Afterwards again read the verses of the Psalm. Repeat bath daily as feel needed. So mote it be.

Psalm 51 v 1-12

1   Have mercy upon me, O God, according to thy loving kindness: according unto the multitude of thy tender mercies blot out my transgressions.

2   Wash me thoroughly from mine iniquity, and cleanse me from my sin.

3   For I acknowledge my transgressions: and my sin is ever before me.

4   Against thee, thee only, have I sinned, and done this evil in thy sight: that thou mightest be justified when thou speakest, and be clear when thou judgest.

5   Behold, I was shapen in iniquity; and in sin did my mother conceive me.

6   Behold, thou desirest truth in the inward parts: and in the hidden part thou shalt make me to know wisdom.

7   Purge me with hyssop, and I shall be clean: wash me, and I shall

be whiter than snow.

8 *Make me to hear joy and gladness; that the bones which thou hast broken may rejoice.*

9 *Hide thy face from my sins, and blot out all mine iniquities.*

10 *Create in me a clean heart, O God; and renew a right spirit within me.*

11 *Cast me not away from thy presence; and take not thy holy spirit from me.*

12 *Restore unto me the joy of thy salvation; and uphold me with thy free spirit.*

~~~~~~~~~~ *** ~~~~~~~~~~

Psalm 119 - Asking forgiveness for one's actions

This is a very powerful working that will set you on the path to standing in the Light of Divinity and receiving all the blessings you deserve. You must be sincere and ready to change/let go of the past or this working could turn onto a curse.

Day: Sunday
Bath Oil: 7 Holy Spirit Hyssop

This is a seven day working. Each morning add 7 Holy Spirit bath oil to your bath. Cleanse yourself completely. When finished read verses of the Psalm aloud several times. So mote it be.

Psalm 119 v169-176

169 *Let my cry come near before thee, O LORD: give me understanding according to thy word.*

170 *Let my supplication come before thee: deliver me according to thy word.*

171 *My lips shall utter praise, when thou hast taught me thy statutes.*

172 *My tongue shall speak of thy word: for all thy commandments*

are righteousness.

173 *Let thine hand help me; for I have chosen thy precepts.*

174 *I have longed for thy salvation, O LORD; and thy law is my delight.*

175 *Let my soul live, and it shall praise thee; and let thy judgments help me.*

176 *I have gone astray like a lost sheep; seek thy servant; for I do not forget thy commandments.*

~~~~~~~~~~ *** ~~~~~~~~~~

Psalm 103 - Seeking forgiveness

When wanting to make peace with the past and start over use this working.

Day: All
Herb: Queen Elizabeth root
Other: Dove's Blood Ink, Parchment paper, red string

Write verses on parchment paper using Dove's Blood ink. Wrap paper around root and secure with red string. Keep with you until feel peace. So mote it be.

Psalm 103 v 1-2-3-12-13-14

1 *Bless the LORD, O my soul: and all that is within me, bless his holy name.*

2 *Bless the LORD, O my soul, and forget not all his benefits:*

3 *Who forgiveth all thine iniquities; who healeth all thy diseases;*

12 *As far as the east is from the west, so far hath he removed our transgressions from us.*

13 *Like as a father pitieth his children, so the LORD pitieth them that fear him. 14 For he knoweth our frame; he remembereth that we are dust.*

~~~~~~~~~~ *** ~~~~~~~~~~

Psalm 135 - Repenting sincerely from sin

When wanting to turn over a new leaf and live your life in the Light of Divinity this working will start you on that path.

Day: All
Incense: 3 Kings
Other: Holy Water

This working needs to start as the first rays of the sun appear in the morning. Light incense. Stand facing the East and say verses of Psalm aloud ending each verse with 'For God is in me and I am in God'. Repeat facing South, East, and North. When done wash hands and feet with Holy Water. Use Psalm 136 working afterwards. So mote it be.

Psalm 135 v 13-14-19-20-21

13 *Thy name, O LORD, endureth forever; and thy memorial, O LORD, throughout all generations.*

14 *For the LORD will judge his people, and he will repent himself concerning his servants.*

19 *Bless the LORD, O house of Israel: bless the LORD, O house of Aaron:*

20 *Bless the LORD, O house of Levi: ye that fear the LORD, bless the LORD.*

21 *Blessed be the LORD out of Zion, which dwelleth at Jerusalem. Praise ye the LORD.*

~~~~~~~~~~ *** ~~~~~~~~~~

Psalm 136 - Forgiveness of sins

The verses of this Psalm create an incredible healing power when used with an open heart and in complete faith. This working is about "getting right with God".

Day: All
Incense: 3 Kings
Other: Holy/Spiritual water

This working can be done right after Psalm 135 working. It is a good idea to use both. Say verses of Psalm aloud with deep meaning and conviction. Next pour Holy Water over top of your head. Stand quietly for a couple of moments and take in all that you have done. Read verses daily for next seven days. So mote it be.

Psalm 136 v 1-7

1   O give thanks unto the LORD; for he is good: for his mercy endureth forever.

2   O give thanks unto the God of gods: for his mercy endureth forever.

3   O give thanks to the Lord of lords: for his mercy endureth forever.

4   To him who alone doeth great wonders: for his mercy endureth forever.

5   To him that by wisdom made the heavens: for his mercy endureth forever.

6   To him that stretched out the earth above the waters: for his mercy endureth forever.

7   To him that made great lights: for his mercy endureth forever:

~~~~~~~~~~ *** ~~~~~~~~~~

Psalm 4 - Making a major decision

Sometimes you need a little extra help when facing a decision that could change your life.

Day: All except Wednesday
Candle: Taper-White
Other: Parchment paper, Dove's Blood Ink
Oil: Success

Anoint candle with Success Oil. Write question on paper with Dove's Blood ink, fold paper in half and place under candle. Light the candle then say the following verse three times. Let the candle burn completely out. When you sleep the answer will come to you. So mote it be.

Psalm 4 v.5
Offer the sacrifices of righteous, and put your trust in the Lord.

~~~~~~~~~~ *** ~~~~~~~~~~

Psalm 40 - Clearing obstacles in your path
Do you feel like there is a wall up every way you turn? Are you always hearing "no" when you know you should be hearing "yes"? This working will help to open the way for you to find your success.

Day: Monday or New Moon
Incense: John the Conqueror
Candle: 7 Day- White
Oil: Success

Light incense. Sit quietly and envision yourself atop a high mountain, the world is at your feet; ready and waiting. When you feel ready light the candle and repeat verses three times. Let candle burn until feel is right then pinch out. For next seven days place a small dab of success oil behind your ears, inside of wrists, and bottoms of feet in morning upon rising. Let candle let burn out completely, do not put out. So mote it be.

Psalm 40 v 13-17

13 Be pleased, O LORD, to deliver me: O LORD, make haste to help me.

14 Let them be ashamed and confounded together that seek after my soul to destroy it; let them be driven backward and put to shame that wish me evil.

15 Let them be desolate for a reward of their shame that say unto me, Aha, aha.

16 Let all those that seek thee rejoice and be glad in thee: let such as love thy salvation say continually, The LORD be magnified.

17 But I am poor and needy; yet the Lord thinketh upon me: thou art my help and my deliverer; make no tarrying, O my God.

~~~~~~~~~~ *** ~~~~~~~~~~

Psalm 49 - Seeking answers

Do you have life changing questions that need to be answered? This working will help to open up that pathway so that the answers come to you when you dream for the next 7 nights.

Day: Wednesday after sunset
Incense: Frankincense-1 tablespoon, Sandalwood-1 tablespoon, Musk powder-1 tablespoon, Wormwood (crushed)- 2 teaspoons, Wood Betony (crushed)-2 tablespoons, Dragon Blood powder-1 teaspoon, Tobacco-1 teaspoon
Oil: Third Eye or Psychic Opener
Other: parchment paper, dragon's blood ink, grave yard dirt, red cloth, fast light charcoal

Combine all incense and blend well. Place 2 tablespoons of mixture on fast light charcoal and light. Add more incense as needed. Anoint candle with oil while saying Psalm 23. On the parchment paper write your question using the dragon's blood ink. On back of paper trace the cross using the oil. Fold paper in half and place under candle. Light the candle and say the verse seven times, slowly and with meaning. Next sprinkle the dirt around base of candle covering the paper while saying "Ancestors and spirits of the past show me the answer I seek." Let candle burn completely out (8" approx. 2 hours). Gather the melted pile-wax, dirt &paper and wrap in red cloth. Place it under your bed at the foot. When you sleep the answer will be revealed. So mote it be.

Psalm 49 v 3

My mouth shall speak of wisdom; and the meditation of my heart shall be of understanding.

~~~~~~~~~~ *** ~~~~~~~~~~

Psalm 80 - Seeking answers

This is a clarity working. Do you feel like there is a cloud of fog around you, stopping you from seeing things clearly and being able to make decisions? This working is very effective in letting you see what or how things really are. Caution: secrets long forgotten may come out. Be prepared.

Day: All
Incense: Frankincense, Myrrh, Sandalwood- equal amounts
Candle: 7 Day-White
Oil: Peace

Anoint candle with Peace oil and light. Burn incense. Sit quietly and clear your mind of all the daily clutter. When feel ready repeat the verse aloud over and over, many, many times until the words seem to blur together. You are building a cone of energy. Now envision all that energy going into you. Take several deep breaths and let what you have created flow all through you. Sit quietly and couple more minutes and when ready, leave. Each day for as long as the candle burns repeat the working. So mote it be.

Psalm 80 v 3

Turn us again, O God, and cause thy face to shine; and we shall be saved.

~~~~~~~~~~ ******* ~~~~~~~~~~

Psalm 84 - Asking for strength

When you feel that bone deep weariness and soul aching need that you can't fill, this is the working to help bring your energies back into balance. Let Divinity's message of love and hope feed your spirit.

Day: All
Herbal Bath: Hyssop Bath Oil/Salt Blend
Candle: Taper-White
Oil: 7 Holy Spirits

This working is best done in the bathroom. Anoint candle with oil and light. Read the verses several times aloud. Take bath/shower and use Hyssop blend bath oils or salt. Cleanse yourself all over, taking your time. Afterwards again read the verses. Pinch out candle. Repeat daily until feel better. So mote it be.

Psalm 84 v 11-12

11 *For the LORD God is a sun and shield: the LORD will give grace and glory: no good thing will he withhold from them that walk uprightly.*

12 *O LORD of hosts, blessed is the man that trusteth in thee.*

~~~~~~~~~~ ******* ~~~~~~~~~~

Psalm 119 - Seeking clarity

When needing to see a matter clearly and looking for the truth. This is very good to use if you believe you are being lied to.

Day: All
Incense: Benzoin
Candle: Taper-Purple
Oil: 7 Holy Spirits
Other: Sea salt, graveyard dirt-handful

This is a three day working that must be done from start to finish in order for it to work. Mix approx. 1 cup salt with graveyard dirt. Use mixture to make a small circle about 2 feet wide. At the East, South, West and North points of circle draw small crosses using remaining mixture. Write your name into the side of candle (a toothpick works well for this) and anoint candle with oil. Place candle in the center of circle and light. Light and place one stick of incense next to each of crosses drawn. Next walk around circle clockwise three times while saying verses of Psalm aloud several times. When done pinch out candle and wipe circle away with a broom. Repeat entire working for next two nights using the same candle. The truth will be revealed to you soon afterwards. So mote it be.

Psalm 119 v 129-136

129 *Thy testimonies are wonderful: therefore doth my soul keep them.*

130 *The entrance of thy words giveth light; it giveth understanding unto the simple.*

131 *I opened my mouth, and panted: for I longed for thy commandments.*

132 *Look thou upon me, and be merciful unto me, as thou usest to do unto those that love thy name.*

133 *Order my steps in thy word: and let not any iniquity have dominion over me. 134 Deliver me from the oppression of man: so will I keep thy precepts.*

135 *Make thy face to shine upon thy servant; and teach me thy statutes.*

136 *Rivers of waters run down mine eyes, because they keep not thy law.*

~~~~~~~~~~ *** ~~~~~~~~~~

Psalm 138 - Seeking confidence

This is a great working to use when needing confidence and to build up your self-esteem. Very good to use when needing to speak up and be heard in any situation.

Day: All
Other: Parchment paper, Bat's blood ink or your own

Write verses of Psalm on parchment paper using Bat's blood ink or your own. Keep the paper with you when need confidence. So mote it be.

Psalm 138 v 7&8

7 *Though I walk in the midst of trouble, thou wilt revive me: thou shalt stretch forth thine hand against the wrath of mine enemies, and thy right hand shall save me.*

8 *The LORD will perfect that which concerneth me: thy mercy, O LORD, endureth forever: forsake not the works of thine own hands.*

~~~~~~~~~~ *** ~~~~~~~~~~

Psalm 148 - Needing direction or guidance

This very good to use when you feel you have too many choices to make a wise decision.

Day: All
Incense: Helping Hand

Burn a little Helping Hand incense and sit quietly reading verses of Psalm as many times as needed. The answers will come soon. So mote it be.

Psalm 148

1   *Praise ye the LORD. Praise ye the LORD from the heavens: praise him in the heights.*

2   *Praise ye him, all his angels: praise ye him, all his hosts.*

3   *Praise ye him, sun and moon: praise him, all ye stars of light.*

4   *Praise him, ye heavens of heavens, and ye waters that be above the heavens.*

5   *Let them praise the name of the LORD: for he commanded, and they were created.*

6   *He hath also established them for ever and ever: he hath made a decree which shall not pass.*

7   *Praise the LORD from the earth, ye dragons, and all deeps:*

8   *Fire, and hail; snow, and vapour; stormy wind fulfilling his word:*

9   *Mountains, and all hills; fruitful trees, and all cedars:*

10 *Beasts, and all cattle; creeping things, and flying fowl:*

11 *Kings of the earth, and all people; princes, and all judges of the earth:*

12 *Both young men, and maidens; old men, and children:*

13 *Let them praise the name of the LORD: for his name alone is excellent; his glory is above the earth and heaven.*

14 *He also exalteth the horn of his people, the praise of all his saints; even of the children of Israel, a people near unto him. Praise ye the LORD.*

10

Wealth-Finances-Business

Honor the Lord with thy substance, and with the first fruits of all thine increase: So shall thy barns be filled with plenty, and thy presses shall burst out with new wines. Proverbs 3:9

Through wisdom a house is built, and by understanding it is established; and by knowledge the rooms shall be filled with all precious and pleasant riches. Proverbs 24:3-4

Magickal Tidbit
Two Ways to Attract Customers/Increase Business
Wash all floors in business with Poke Root tincture.
Place nine straight pins in fresh whole Garlic. Hang with red thread over business doorway.

~~~~~~~~~~ *** ~~~~~~~~~~

Psalm 34 - Prosperity to keep blessings coming
When things are going well this prayer will help to insure that all stays that way.

Day: All
Candle-High John the Conqueror
Other: High John the Conqueror root, white cotton cloth, $1 bill, red thread

Light the candle and slowly with purpose say all the verses aloud. After each verse say "And the blessings continue." Wrap $1 bill around root and secure with red thread. Place root as close to center in your house (a closet or under sink in bathroom/kitchen, some place out of sight). Be creative. So mote it be.

Psalm 34 v 12-16

12   *What man is he that desireth life, and loveth many days, that he may see good?*

13   *Keep thy tongue from evil, and thy lips from speaking guile.*

14   *Depart from evil, and do good; seek peace, and pursue it.*

15   *The eyes of the LORD are upon the righteous, and his ears are open unto their cry.*

16   *The face of the LORD is against them that do evil, to cut off the remembrance of them from the earth.*

~~~~~~~~~~ *** ~~~~~~~~~~

Psalm 68 - Attracting wealth

This working is for long term goals. It is very good to do when starting a new business or job. Use this to set yourself up for what you deserve.

Day: All
Herb: High John the Conqueror Root-3 pieces
Candle: High John the Conqueror
Other: a dollar bill, piece of string or rubber band

Wrap the dollar bill around 1 piece of High John the Conqueror Root, secure with string or rubber band. Keep this with you at all times; carry in your pocket or purse. Let no one touch it. Light the High John the Conqueror candle and say the verses of the Psalm daily while candle is lit (approx. seven days). After saying verses take another piece of High John the Conqueror Root and roll around in your hands while concentrating on your goals. Place this piece under the foot of your bed. Take the third piece of High John the Conqueror Root and boil in a quart of rain or spring boil. When cooled sprinkle in all corners of your house. Rub your hands and feet with mixture. Also dab on center of your forehead daily while candle burns. So mote it be.

Psalm 68 v 13-19

13   *Though ye have lien among the pots, yet shall ye be as the wings of a dove covered with silver, and her feathers with yellow gold.*

14   *When the Almighty scattered kings in it, it was white as snow in Salmon.*

15   *The hill of God is as the hill of Bashan; an high hill as the hill of Bashan.*

16   *Why leap ye, ye high hills? this is the hill which God desireth to dwell in; yea, the LORD will dwell in it forever.*

17   *The chariots of God are twenty thousand, even thousands of angels: the Lord is among them, as in Sinai, in the holy place.*

18   *Thou hast ascended on high, thou hast led captivity captive: thou hast received gifts for men; yea, for the rebellious also, that the LORD God might dwell among them.*

19   *Blessed be the Lord, who daily loadeth us with benefits, even the God of our salvation. Selah.*

~ ~ ~ ~ ~ ~ ~ ~ ~ ~ ******* ~ ~ ~ ~ ~ ~ ~ ~ ~ ~

Psalm 72 - Increasing wealth

Help to insure that your money grows and multiplies using this working. Good for lotteries, bingo and games of chance.

Day: Friday
Herb: High John the Conqueror root
Oil: Money
Other: $1.00 bill, rubber band

Anoint root with money oil. Wrap $1.00 bill around it and secure with rubber band. While holding root in your hands read aloud the two verses seven times. Keep root with you at all times. So mote it be.

Psalm 72 v1&7

1   *Give the king thy judgments, O God, and thy righteousness unto the king's son.*

7   *In his days shall the righteous flourish; and abundance of peace so long as the moon endureth.*

~~~~~~~~~~ ***** ~~~~~~~~~~

Psalm 107 - Obtaining a desired item

You saw it, you want it, you must have it. This working will aid you in getting what you desire. Not to be used for obtaining money or love.

Day: All
Herb: Solomon's Seal powder
Candle: Taper-Black
Other: Solomon's Seal

Write what you desire into the wax of the candle. Place candle on top of Solomon's Seal and light. Burn Solomon's Seal powder and say verses of Psalm aloud. Let candle burn completely until pile of wax. Form ball of wax around Seal and throw into moving river or stream. So mote it be.

Psalm 107 v 28-30

28   *Then they cry unto the LORD in their trouble, and he bringeth them out of their distresses.*

29   *He maketh the storm a calm, so that the waves thereof are still.*

30   *Then are they glad because they be quiet; so he bringeth them unto their desired haven.*

~~~~~~~~~~ ***** ~~~~~~~~~~

Psalm 113 - Winning prizes/drawings

Increase your chances of winning in lotteries and drawings by keeping this powerful mojo bag with you. Also good for bingo.

Day: All
Incense: Bayberry
Herb: Buckeye Root-small piece, Beth Root-small piece
Oil: Gambling and/or Bingo
Other: small red cotton/flannel bag, charm/pendant of dollar sign ($)-or you can write dollar sign on small piece of parchment paper, 7 strands of your hair

When saying this Psalm change "him" to "me" in verse 8. Burn incense in space using to create mojo bag. Assemble all items (7 strands of your hair, Buckeye Root, Beth Root, $ pendant) on table in front of you. For each item-anoint with oil, hold in both hands while saying verses of Psalm aloud, place in bag. When all items are in the bag tie/sew shut. Keep with you when gambling. Do not let other people know you have a mojo bag or touch it. If this happens the mojo is no good. Throw it away and make another one. So mote it be.

Psalms 113 v 1-2-3-7-8-9

1 *Praise ye the LORD. Praise, O ye servants of the LORD, praise the name of the LORD.*

2 *Blessed be the name of the LORD from this time forth and for evermore.*

3 *From the rising of the sun unto the going down of the same the LORD'S name is to be praised.*

7 *He raiseth up the poor out of the dust, and lifteth the needy out of the dunghill;*

8 *That he may set him with princes, even with the princes of his people.*

9 *He maketh the barren woman to keep house, and to be a joyful*

mother of children. Praise ye the LORD.

~~~~~~~~~~ ******* ~~~~~~~~~~

Psalm 72 - Help paying bills

When you find yourself in a time of need through no fault of your own use this working to lift your voice to Divinity for help. Faith that all things are possible is needed for this working. All you have to do is believe.

Day: All
Herb: Jezebel root
Candle: Green taper
Oil: Money

Start this working right after the last rays of the sun have gone. Light the candle and let completely burn until have a palm size clump of melted wax. Form a ball with wax and poke root all the way through the center. Anoint ball with money oil.

After midnight take ball to graveyard and bury behind a tombstone. When filling in the hole repeat the verses aloud. Make sure no one can tell anything was buried. Walk away and don't look back. So mote it be.

Psalm 72 v 12-18

12 *For he shall deliver the needy when he crieth; the poor also, and him that hath no helper.*

13 *He shall spare the poor and needy, and shall save the souls of the needy.*

14 *He shall redeem their soul from deceit and violence: and precious shall their blood be in his sight.*

15 *And he shall live, and to him shall be given of the gold of Sheba: prayer also shall be made for him continually; and daily shall he be praised.*

16   There shall be an handful of corn in the earth upon the top of the mountains; the fruit thereof shall shake like Lebanon: and they of the city shall flourish like grass of the earth.

17   His name shall endure forever: his name shall be continued as long as the sun: and men shall be blessed in him: all nations shall call him blessed.

18   Blessed be the LORD God, the God of Israel, who only doeth wondrous things.

~~~~~~~~~~ *** ~~~~~~~~~~

Psalm 119 - Help to pay a bill or debt

Use when you have a bill or debt come due that you are having problems paying.

Day: All
Herb: Cinnamon
Candle: High John the Conqueror
Oil: Money
Other: High John the Conqueror Root, copy of bill or amount of debt written on a piece of parchment paper

Anoint candle with oil. Light the candle and place bill under candle. Read verses of the Psalms aloud. Rub cinnamon and money oil on High John root while again saying verses of the Psalm. Keep root with you until debt is paid. So mote it be.

Psalm 119 v 17-19-21-24

17   Deal bountifully with thy servant, that I may live, and keep thy word.

19   I am a stranger in the earth: hide not thy commandments from me.

21   Thou hast rebuked the proud that are cursed, which do err from thy commandments.

24   *Thy testimonies also are my delight and my counsellors.*

~~~~~~~~~~ *** ~~~~~~~~~~

Psalm 107 - Getting out of poverty

Sometimes hard work and desire is not enough to make a change in finances. Use this working to help move things along.

Day: All
Candle: 7 Day-High John the Conqueror

Light the candle and say verses of Psalm daily for as long as candle burns. So mote it be.

Psalm107 v 41-42-43

41   *Yet setteth he the poor on high from affliction, and maketh him families like a flock.*

42   *The righteous shall see it, and rejoice: and all iniquity shall stop her mouth.*

43   *Who so is wise, and will observe these things, even they shall understand the loving kindness of the LORD.*

~~~~~~~~~~ *** ~~~~~~~~~~

Psalm 119 - Seeking wisdom regarding finances

Use this wonderful working to help you tune in and listen to the voice of Divinity that is within us all. Very useful when feeling undecided or facing a big decision regarding finances.

Day: Full Moon
Herbal: Incense-Solomon's Seal powder-1 teaspoon, Wormwood-3 teaspoons, Frankincense-4 teaspoons, Sandalwood-6 teaspoons, Vetivert powder-2 teaspoons, Wood Betony-1 cup, Saltpeter-1/2 teaspoon

Candle: 7 Day-Black Double Action

Mix herbs together and store in an airtight container. Mixture is good for about 60 days. Burn 2-3 tablespoons of herbal mixture and light the candle. Sit in front of candle and read verses of Psalm aloud several times. Leave candle to burn. Repeat this for two more days. It is said on the third day you will know that which you seek. So mote it be.

Psalm 119 v97-100 & 104

97   *O how love I thy law! it is my meditation all the day.*

98   *Thou through thy commandments hast made me wiser than mine enemies: for they are ever with me.*

99   *I have more understanding than all my teachers: for thy testimonies are my meditation.*

100 *I understand more than the ancients, because I keep thy precepts.*

104 *Through thy precepts I get understanding: therefore I hate every false way.*

~~~~~~~~~~ ******* ~~~~~~~~~~

Psalm 71 - Increase business growth

When wanting to make your business more profitable and to attract new customers this working will help you to achieve those goals.

Day: All
Candle: 7 Day-Yellow
Oil: Money drawing
Incense: John the Conqueror, Echinacea powder, Allspice, Clove, Angelica
Other: Sea salt

Start this working at sunrise on your chosen day. Mix equal amounts of John the Conqueror, Echinacea, Allspice, Clove, and Angelica powder. Store mixture in an air tight container in a cool dark area. On the first day anoint candle with money drawing oil and light. Burn small amount (approx. 1 teaspoon) of incense mixture.

Say aloud verses three times. At sunset again burn incense mixture and say verses three times. Do this for seven days or as long as candle burns. Sprinkle small amount of sea salt in all corners of business or shop. If you work from home sprinkle salt in all corners of house. So mote it be.

Psalm 71 v 1-2-3-7-21

1   *In thee, O Lord, do I put my trust: let me never be put to confusion.*

2   *Deliver me in thy righteousness, and cause me to escape: incline thine ear unto me, and save me.*

3   *Be thou my strong habitation, whereunto I may continually resort: thou hast given commandment to save me; for thou art my rock and my fortress.*

7   *I am as a wonder unto many; but thou art my strong refuge.*

21   *Thou shalt increase my greatness, and comfort me on every side.*

~~~~~~~~~~ *** ~~~~~~~~~~

Psalm 108 - Increasing business

Are you wanting to expand and have growth in your business? Let this working make success a reality. Good for when you are having a sale or special event as well.

Day: All
Incense: money drawing, John the Conqueror
Candle: Taper-Pink

Oil: money oil
Other: 7 shiny pennies

Anoint candle with oil and light. Place pennies in a circle around the candle. Burn incense and say verses of Psalm aloud several times until feel satisfied. Repeat as feel necessary. Pinch out candle, can be used again. Place pennies in cash register. So mote it be.

Psalm 108 v 1-2-3

1   *O God, my heart is fixed; I will sing and give praise, even with my glory.*
2   *Awake, psaltery and harp: I myself will awake early.*
3   *I will praise thee, O LORD, among the people: and I will sing praises unto thee among the nations.*

~~~~~~~~~~ *** ~~~~~~~~~~

Psalm 122 - Increasing business

This is another very simple and effective working to help your business increase.

Day: All
Other: Parchment paper, Dragon's blood ink

Write verse on paper using Dragon's blood ink and place in your cash register or money box. So mote it be.

Psalm 122 v 7

7   *Peace be within thy walls, and prosperity within thy palaces.*

~~~~~~~~~~ *** ~~~~~~~~~~

Psalm 79 - Being wronged in business

When a business dealing has gone wrong, people didn't keep their word, or money was not fairly exchanged this working will give seven years of bad luck to the person responsible.

Day: Full Moon
Incense: Crossing & Dragon's Blood-equal amounts
Candle: Taper-Black
Oil: JuJu
Other: Dove's Blood ink, parchment paper

Start this working on the first night of the full moon after midnight. Write enemies' name seven times on parchment paper using Dove's Blood ink. Sprinkle paper with JuJu oil. Place paper under black taper candle and light the candle. Burn incense close by. Let candle burn completely out. Take wax and paper and form a ball with it. Find a fast moving river and throw wax ball into it. Afterwards, stand facing river and say aloud the verses of the Psalm. When done leave immediately and don't look back. So mote it be.

Psalm 79 v 6-13

6   *Pour out thy wrath upon the heathen that have not known thee, and upon the kingdoms that have not called upon thy name.*

7   *For they have devoured Jacob, and laid waste his dwelling place.*

8   *O remember not against us former iniquities: let thy tender mercies speedily prevent us: for we are brought very low.*

9   *Help us, O God of our salvation, for the glory of thy name: and deliver us, and purge away our sins, for thy name's sake.*

10 *Wherefore should the heathen say, Where is their God? let him be known among the heathen in our sight by the revenging of the blood of thy servants which is shed.*

11 *Let the sighing of the prisoner come before thee; according to the greatness of thy power preserve thou those that are appointed to*

die;

12 *And render unto our neighbours sevenfold into their bosom their reproach, wherewith they have reproached thee, O Lord.*

13 *So we thy people and sheep of thy pasture will give thee thanks for ever: we will shew forth thy praise to all generations.*

11

Evil Influences-Lying-Gossip

Be not overcome of evil, but overcome evil with good. Romans 12:21

Those who consider themselves religious and yet do not keep a tight rein on their tongues deceive themselves, and their religion is worthless. James 1:26

Magickal Tidbit
Put slippery elm in a small red bag and keep in your pocket to ward off evil doers.

~~~~~~~~~~ *** ~~~~~~~~~~

Psalm 18 - Staying in the light of God when evil is near
To keep you safe in the light of Divinity when evil is near.

Day: All
Incense: Angelica powder
Candle: Taper-White
Other: Red cotton bag, small cross, holy water or spring water that has not been in a metal pipe

Light incense and candle. Read aloud all verses. Wash cross in water and place in red bag. Place it under your mattress. You may either let the candle burn out completely or you may pinch it out. It is your choice. Do what feels right. So mote it be.

Psalm 18 v. 2-6-20-21-27-28-35-36
2   *The LORD is my rock, and my fortress, and my deliverer; my God, my strength, in whom I will trust; my buckler, and the*

horn of my salvation, and my high tower.

6   *In my distress I called upon the LORD, and cried unto my God: he heard my voice out of his temple, and my cry came before him, even into his ears.*

20   *The LORD rewarded me according to my righteousness; according to the cleanness of my hands hath he recompensed me.*

21   *For I have kept the ways of the LORD, and have not wickedly departed from my God.*

27   *For thou wilt save the afflicted people; but wilt bring down high looks.*

28   *For thou wilt light my candle: the LORD my God will enlighten my darkness.*

35   *Thou hast also given me the shield of thy salvation: and thy right hand hath holden me up, and thy gentleness hath made me great.*

36   *Thou hast enlarged my steps under me that my feet did not slip.*

~~~~~~~~~~ *** ~~~~~~~~~~

Psalm 73 - Stopping envious/jealous thoughts

Envy and jealously have been the downfall of many, don't let that happen to you. Let the Spirit of Divinity help give you the security that you need.

Day: Sunday
Incense: Mystic Rites, Powdered Peace
Herb: Patchouli

This is a three day working that needs to begin on Sunday after midnight. It is very important to prepare yourself properly by taking a good cleansing bath/shower before starting. When ready sprinkle the patchouli on the ground creating a six foot circle. Place/burn incense in the east of the circle. Stand in the center of circle facing the east. Hold your head high and use a strong voice to say all of the verses aloud. Repeat working for next two nights again waiting until after midnight start. On the third night you should feel differently; if you do not repeat working again. So mote it be.

Psalm 73

1   *Truly God is good to Israel, even to such as are of a clean heart.*

2   *But as for me, my feet were almost gone; my steps had well nigh slipped.*

3   *For I was envious at the foolish, when I saw the prosperity of the wicked.*

4   *For there are no bands in their death: but their strength is firm.*

5   *They are not in trouble as other men; neither are they plagued like other men.*

6   *Therefore pride compasseth them about as a chain; violence covereth them as a garment.*

7   *Their eyes stand out with fatness: they have more than heart could wish.*

8   *They are corrupt, and speak wickedly concerning oppression: they speak loftily.*

9   *They set their mouth against the heavens, and their tongue walketh through the earth.*

10 *Therefore his people return hither: and waters of a full cup are wrung out to them.*

11 *And they say, How doth God know? and is there knowledge in the most High?*

12 *Behold, these are the ungodly, who prosper in the world; they increase in riches.*

13 *Verily I have cleansed my heart in vain, and washed my hands in innocency.*

14 *For all the day long have I been plagued, and chastened every morning.*

15 *If I say, I will speak thus; behold, I should offend against the*

generation of thy children.

16 When I thought to know this, it was too painful for me;

17 Until I went into the sanctuary of God; then understood I their end.

18 Surely thou didst set them in slippery places: thou castedst them down into destruction.

19 How are they brought into desolation, as in a moment! they are utterly consumed with terrors.

20 As a dream when one awaketh; so, O Lord, when thou awakest, thou shalt despise their image.

21 Thus my heart was grieved, and I was pricked in my reins.

22 So foolish was I, and ignorant: I was as a beast before thee.

23 Nevertheless I am continually with thee: thou hast holden me by my right hand.

24 Thou shalt guide me with thy counsel, and afterward receive me to glory.

25 Whom have I in heaven but thee? and there is none upon earth that I desire beside thee.

26 My flesh and my heart faileth: but God is the strength of my heart, and my portion forever.

27 For, lo, they that are far from thee shall perish: thou hast destroyed all them that go a whoring from thee.

28 But it is good for me to draw near to God: I have put my trust in the Lord GOD, that I may declare all thy works.

~~~~~~~~~~ *** ~~~~~~~~~~

Psalm 100 - Overcoming all evil influences

Use this working to rid yourself of evil spirits and bad influences that may be the cause of bad luck, lack of wealth/opportunities or laziness.

Day: All
Oil: Cast Off Evil, Blessing or Divinity

Candles: Taper-Black & White
Other: Parchment paper

Anoint black candle with Cast Off Evil oil and white candle with Blessing or Divinity oil. Write person's name on parchment paper and place under white candle. Light both candles and read the verses aloud. Let candles burn completely. So mote it be.

Psalm 100

1   *Make a joyful noise unto the LORD, all ye lands.*
2   *Serve the LORD with gladness: come before his presence with singing.*
3   *Know ye that the LORD he is God: it is he that hath made us, and not we ourselves; we are his people, and the sheep of his pasture.*
4   *Enter into his gates with thanksgiving, and into his courts with praise: be thankful unto him, and bless his name.*
5   *For the LORD is good; his mercy is everlasting; and his truth endureth to all generations.*

~~~~~~~~~~ ******* ~~~~~~~~~~

Psalm 118 - Stopping dark or evil forces

Surround yourself in the Light of Divinity when you know that evil is near. Very good working when you know someone has sent something dark your way. Said to be an excellent barrier against the undead.

Day: All
Herb: Barberry, Comfrey bark-1/2 cup each
Other: Crushed red brick, sea salt-1/2 cup each

Blend herbs, crushed red brick and salt together. Take mixture and lightly sprinkle across all doorways and windows. Also sprinkle under all beds. While doing this say verses of Psalm aloud. When finished open front door and say verse 26 aloud three times, shut door firmly. So mote it be.

Psalm 118 v 14-26

14 *The LORD is my strength and song, and is become my salvation.*

15 *The voice of rejoicing and salvation is in the tabernacles of the righteous: the right hand of the LORD doeth valiantly.*

16 *The right hand of the LORD is exalted: the right hand of the LORD doeth valiantly.*

17 *I shall not die, but live, and declare the works of the LORD.*

18 *The LORD hath chastened me sore: but he hath not given me over unto death. 19 Open to me the gates of righteousness: I will go into them, and I will praise the LORD:*

20 *This gate of the LORD, into which the righteous shall enter.*

21 *I will praise thee: for thou hast heard me, and art become my salvation.*

22 *The stone which the builders refused is become the head stone of the corner. 23 This is the LORD'S doing; it is marvellous in our eyes.*

24 *This is the day which the LORD hath made; we will rejoice and be glad in it. 25 Save now, I beseech thee, O LORD: O LORD, I beseech thee, send now prosperity.*

26 *Blessed be he that cometh in the name of the LORD: we have blessed you out of the house of the LORD.*

~~~~~~~~~~ *** ~~~~~~~~~~

Psalm 119 - Being surrounded by evil people

Do not let the evil of other people influence or affect you. This is an excellent protection working that is still very popular today.

Day: All
Oil: Protection

Incense: Blood Root, Mullien-equal amounts
Herb: Devil's Shoe String-1 piece
Candle: 7 Day-Protection
Other: parchment paper Angel Raphael

Burn incense mixture. Anoint candle, Devil's Shoe String, corners of parchment paper and self with oil. Write the angel Raphael's name seven times on parchment paper. Fold paper and place under candle. Place Devil's Shoe String so that it is touching the candle and the paper. Light the candle and say verses of Psalm aloud. When candle is done keep Devil's Shoe String on you when you know evil people are near. So mote it be.

Psalm 119 v49-56

49   *Remember the word unto thy servant, upon which thou hast caused me to hope.*

50   *This is my comfort in my affliction: for thy word hath quickened me.*

51   *The proud have had me greatly in derision: yet have I not declined from thy law.*

52   *I remembered thy judgments of old, O LORD; and have comforted myself.*

53   *Horror hath taken hold upon me because of the wicked that forsake thy law.*

54   *Thy statutes have been my songs in the house of my pilgrimage.*

55   *I have remembered thy name, O LORD, in the night, and have kept thy law.*

56   *This I had, because I kept thy precepts.*

~~~~~~~~~~ ***** ~~~~~~~~~~

Psalm 131 - Being possessed by the evil spirit of pride
Pride can be the downfall of many a good person. Don't let this happen to you.

Day: All

Do not let the simplicity of this working fool you. Use the power of the words in this Psalm to help you rid of any false pride that you may have. Sit quietly and read the verses aloud several times until feel a calmness come over you. So mote it be.

Psalm 131

1 LORD, my heart is not haughty, nor mine eyes lofty: neither do I exercise myself in great matters, or in things too high for me.

2 Surely I have behaved and quieted myself, as a child that is weaned of his mother: my soul is even as a weaned child.

3 Let Israel hope in the LORD from henceforth and forever.

~~~~~~~~~~ *** ~~~~~~~~~~

Psalm 137 - Releasing oneself from hate, envy or malice

"May my enemies come to my door so I may feed them." Let go of the dark emotions, thoughts, and energies with this working. When we are able to love our enemies then we may stand in the wondrous Light of God.

Day: All
Incense: equal parts Frankincense and Myrrh
Other: Honey, milk

Find a large oak tree. On the north facing side pour milk and honey on the ground while saying verses of Psalm aloud. Light incense and sit quietly for a few moments. Again say verses of Psalm aloud. So mote it be.

Psalm 137 v 1-6

1 By the rivers of Babylon, there we sat down, yea, we wept, when

we remembered Zion.

2   *We hanged our harps upon the willows in the midst thereof.*

3   *For there they that carried us away captive required of us a song; and they that wasted us required of us mirth, saying, sing us one of the songs of Zion.*

4   *How shall we sing the LORD'S song in a strange land?*

5   *If I forget thee, O Jerusalem, let my right hand forget her cunning.*

6   *If I do not remember thee, let my tongue cleave to the roof of my mouth; if I prefer not Jerusalem above my chief joy.*

~~~~~~~~~~ *** ~~~~~~~~~~

Psalm 63 - Stopping someone from spreading lies about you

When the lies of someone are hurting you, use this working to stop them from speaking against you.

Day: All
Incense: John the Conqueror
Herb: Nettles-2 tablespoons
Candle: Taper-White
Oil: John the Conqueror
Other: Seal of Mephistophilis

Using a pencil write/crave the verse of the Psalm into the candle. Anoint candle with oil. Put Nettles in a small pile with candle in center. Light the candle and let burn completely out. Form a ball using melted wax and nettles. Take ball to a strongly flowing river and throw in. Immediately turn your back and walk away. Do NOT look back. Burn incense for next seven days. Keep the Seal of Mephistopheles on your person at all times. So mote it be.

Psalm 63 v 11

11 But the king shall rejoice in God; every one that sweareth by him shall glory: but the mouth of them that speak lies shall be stopped.

~~~~~~~~~~ *** ~~~~~~~~~~

Psalm 119 - Stopping people from lying about you

When you know the person/s identity who is lying or spreading untruths about you use this working to stop them.

Day: Wednesday
Herb: Nettles
Candle: Taper-Black
Oil: Shut up
Other: black doll, parchment paper

Write person's name on paper three times and put paper in doll with nettles. Anoint mouth of doll and candle with shut up oil. Light the candle and place doll in front of candle. Say verses aloud several times while concentrating on the person/s. When finished wrap doll in plain brown paper and hide in a safe place. Destroy doll when no longer needed. So mote it be.

Psalm 120 v 1 &2

1   *In my distress I cried unto the LORD, and he heard me.*
2   *Deliver my soul, O LORD, from lying lips, and from a deceitful tongue.*

~~~~~~~~~~ *** ~~~~~~~~~~

Psalm 140 - Punishing liars

When the lies of someone have caused hurt or pain to others, use this working to return all that they have created back upon them. Very effective and destructive, make sure the person truly deserves this.

Day: All
Incense: John the Conqueror
Candle: Taper-Black
Herb: Chicory-2 tablespoons
Other: Four Thieves Vinegar, War Water, Dove's Blood ink, parchment paper, sea salt

This is a 2 day working that needs to be done right after midnight on both days. On the first night using Dove's blood ink write person's name on parchment paper three times. In a bowl mix Chicory and 1 cup War Water. Place paper in bowl and soak overnight. Say verses of Psalm aloud while holding bowl. Next morning take paper out of war water and let dry. Save water so can be used later. On second night cleanse your space that you are doing the working in. Make a small circle using sea salt. Place paper in center with black candle on top of it. Light the candle and say verses of Psalm aloud three times. Sprinkle Four Thieves Vinegar around circle careful not to touch candle or paper. Take paper from under candle and pass through flame several times. Then crumple paper in a tight ball and bury in dirt. Pour War Water on top. So mote it be.

Psalm 140 v6-8-10-11

6   *I said unto the LORD, Thou art my God: hear the voice of my supplications, O LORD.*

8   *Grant not, O LORD, the desires of the wicked: further not his wicked device; lest they exalt themselves. Selah.*

10 *Let burning coals fall upon them: let them be cast into the fire; into deep pits that they rise not up again.*

11 *Let not an evil speaker be established in the earth: evil shall hunt the violent man to overthrow him.*

~~~~~~~~~~ *** ~~~~~~~~~~

Psalm 27 - Stopping people from gossiping about you

When you find yourself surrounded by people who spend their time gossiping, use this working so they don't speak of you.

Day: All
Candle: Taper-Pink
Oil: High John
Other: Evil Eye pendant

Light the candle. While saying verses rub High John oil on pendant. Let candle burn awhile then pinch out. Keep/wear pendant close to you when gossipers are near. So mote it be.

Psalm 27 v 1-6

1 *The LORD is my light and my salvation; whom shall I fear? The LORD is the strength of my life; of whom shall I be afraid?*

2 *When the wicked, even mine enemies and my foes, came upon me to eat up my flesh, they stumbled and fell.*

3 *Though an host should encamp against me, my heart shall not fear: though war should rise against me, in this will I be confident.*

4 *One thing have I desired of the LORD, that will I seek after; that I may dwell in the house of the LORD all the days of my life, to behold the beauty of the LORD, and to enquire in his temple.*

5 *For in the time of trouble he shall hide me in his pavilion: in the secret of his tabernacle shall he hide me; he shall set me up upon a rock.*

6 *And now shall mine head be lifted up above mine enemies round about me: therefore will I offer in his tabernacle sacrifices of joy; I will sing, yea, I will sing praises unto the LORD.*

~~~~~~~~~~ *** ~~~~~~~~~~

Psalm 36 - Turning gossip into compliments

This is a great way to help you become popular or to insure that people are only saying good things about you.

Day: Saturday
Candle: Taper-Green
Oil: Attraction
Herbal Bath: Quince seed (crushed)-1 tsp., Lemon Verbena powder-1 tsp. (dried-1 tbl.), Queen of the Meadow-1 tsp., Calamus powder 1 tsp. (dried 1 tbl.)
Other: 1 gallon spring water

Combine all herbs and place in small cotton bag. Put bag in water and place container in cool dark place for seven days. Now is ready to use for bath or final rinse in shower. Use approx. ½ cup for each bath/shower. For the next eight days use every day when take bath. After taking the first bath rub candle with oil while saying all the verses. Light the candle and repeat all the verses two more times. Let candle burn until feels right and then pinch out. Continue using herbal bath for next eight days. So mote it be.

Psalm 36 v 2-3-8

2   *For he flattereth himself in his own eyes, until his iniquity be found to be hateful.*

3   *The words of his mouth are iniquity and deceit: he hath left off to be wise, and to do good.*

8   *They shall be abundantly satisfied with the fatness of thy house; and thou shalt make them drink of the river of thy pleasures.*

12

Travel-Work-School

For He guards the course of the just and protects the way of his faithful ones.
Proverbs 2:8

Apply your heart to instruction and your ears to words of knowledge.
Proverbs 23:12

Magickal Tidbit
Broom Magick
Never bring an old broom into a new house.
Put a broom under the bed to ward off bad dreams.
Sweep house on a New Moon to rid of old energies.

~~~~~~~~~~ *** ~~~~~~~~~~

Psalm 116 - Safe travel
When you have to travel on a regular basis this working will create a powerful protection charm for you to use.

Day: All
Herb: Mugwort-2 teaspoons
Oil: Lodestone
Other: Planet Mars Talisman, small red cotton/flannel bag

Anoint Seal with oil while reading verses of Psalm. Place Seal and herbs in bag and secure. Keep the bag with you when traveling to insure safety and peace. So mote it be.

Psalm 116 v 9-19

9   *I will walk before the LORD in the land of the living.*

10   *I believed, therefore have I spoken: I was greatly afflicted:*

11   *I said in my haste, All men are liars.*

12   *What shall I render unto the LORD for all his benefits toward me?*

13   *I will take the cup of salvation, and call upon the name of the LORD.*

14   *I will pay my vows unto the LORD now in the presence of all his people.*

15   *Precious in the sight of the LORD is the death of his saints.*

16   *O LORD, truly I am thy servant; I am thy servant, and the son of thine handmaid: thou hast loosed my bonds.*

17   *I will offer to thee the sacrifice of thanksgiving, and will call upon the name of the LORD.*

18   *I will pay my vows unto the LORD now in the presence of all his people,*

19   *In the courts of the LORD'S house, in the midst of thee, O Jerusalem. Praise ye the LORD.*

~~~~~~~~~~ *** ~~~~~~~~~~

Psalm 121 - Safe travel

This is a very simple and effective working to help keep you safe when you must travel. Very good for people with long commutes and helping to keep transportation reliable.

Day: All
Other: Parchment paper, Dragon's blood ink

Write verses on paper using Dragon's blood ink. Keep the paper with you when traveling. So mote it be.

Psalm 121 v 5-8

5   *The LORD is thy keeper: the LORD is thy shade upon thy right hand.*

6   *The sun shall not smite thee by day, nor the moon by night.*

7   *The LORD shall preserve thee from all evil: he shall preserve thy soul.*

8   *The LORD shall preserve thy going out and thy coming in from this time forth, and even for evermore.*

~~~~~~~~~~ *** ~~~~~~~~~~

Psalm 119 - Safety when traveling to a new place

This working will create a Talisman to keep with you that will help to insure your safety while traveling or visiting new places. This working is one of the best examples of pure American Hoodoo- blending European and African magick.

Day: Full Moon
Incense: Dragon's Blood
Oil: Protection
Other: Parchment paper, Dragon's Blood ink, red string, black chicken feather

Draw a large "eye" on paper using feather as a pen with Dragon's Blood ink. Burn incense and pass paper several times through the smoke. Anoint corners of paper with Protection oil. On other side of paper write verse 105 down. Fold paper three times and bind with red string while sayings the following aloud: "Three times three will be sacred to thee. nine times said will bind it tight making it right." Next put paper talisman in both hands while saying the verses of the Psalm nine times. Say aloud-over and over putting your energy into the talisman you have just created. When finished keep talisman with you when traveling. Let no one touch it. So mote it be.

Psalm 119 v 105 &106

105 *Thy word is a lamp unto my feet, and a light unto my path.*

106 *I have sworn, and I will perform it, that I will keep thy righteous judgments.*

~~~~~~~~~~ *** ~~~~~~~~~~

Psalm 124 - Safety when traveling by boat

This very powerful Psalm is a Song of David. It has been used successfully for centuries by those that need safe passage or work on a boat. Very good for fishermen/women.

Day: All
Oil: Blessings
Other: Parchment paper, Dragon's blood ink

Write Psalms on paper using Dragon's blood ink, anoint corners with oil. Fold paper three times and keep with you when on boat. So mote it be.

Psalm 124

1   *If it had not been the LORD who was on our side, now may Israel say;*

2   *If it had not been the LORD who was on our side, when men rose up against us:*

3   *Then they had swallowed us up quick, when their wrath was kindled against us:*

4   *Then the waters had overwhelmed us, the stream had gone over our soul:*

5   *Then the proud waters had gone over our soul.*

6   *Blessed be the LORD, who hath not given us as a prey to their teeth.*

7   *Our soul is escaped as a bird out of the snare of the fowlers: the snare is broken, and we are escaped.*

8   *Our help is in the name of the LORD, who made heaven and earth.*

~~~~~~~~~~ ***** ~~~~~~~~~~

Psalm 27 - Success in new situations

Are you nervous, anxious or fearful about trying something new? Have a new job? Needing to impress people? Use this prayer to unleash the confidence that is within you.

Day: All
Incense: 3 teaspoons Wood Betony, ½ cup Frankincense, 2 teaspoons Orris root powder, 1 cup Sandalwood, ½ teaspoon Saltpeter
Oil: Success
Candle: Taper-White
Other: Turquoise stone-better if can part of necklace or bracelet, Holy Water

Combine all incense and burn. Light the candle while saying all verses. Wash Turquoise stone(s) with Holy water and rub with oil again while saying verses. Hold stone(s) in your hand and again slowly repeat all verses. Wear or put stone(s) in pocket whenever having to speak publicly. So mote it be.

Psalm 27 v 1-2-3

1   *The LORD is my light and my salvation; whom shall I fear? The LORD is the strength of my life; of whom shall I be afraid?*

2   *When the wicked, even mine enemies and my foes, came upon me to eat up my flesh, they stumbled and fell.*

3   *Though an host should encamp against me, my heart shall not fear: though war should rise against me, in this will I be confident.*

~~~~~~~~~~ *** ~~~~~~~~~~

Psalm 75 - Job promotion

Need your boss to see your real worth? Wanting to get the salary you deserve? Use this working to help achieve that goal.

Day: All
Herb: powdered Red Clover
Other: Lodestone, small red cotton bag, parchment paper, bat's blood ink

Write verses on parchment paper using bat's blood ink. Fold paper three times and place in red cotton bag. Put approx. 2 teaspoons of red clover powder and lodestone in bag and sew or tie securely shut. Keep bag with you at all times when at work, either in your pocket or around your neck as a necklace. So mote it be.

Psalm 75 v 6-7

6   For promotion cometh neither from the east, nor from the west, nor from the south.

7   But God is the judge: he putteth down one, and setteth up another.

~~~~~~~~~~ *** ~~~~~~~~~~

Psalm 119 - Looking for work

The best way to get a job quick is to work both the astral world and the physical world. This working will insure the astral world lines up in your favor. In the physical world you must let everyone know you are looking for a job and fill out as many applications as you can.

Day: All
Herb: Devil's Shoe String-1 piece

Candle: Job
Oil-Nutmeg, Vanilla

Anoint candle, Devil's Shoe String and self with both Nutmeg and Vanilla oils. Light the candle and place Devil's Shoe String in front of candle. Read verses of Psalm. Keep Devil's Shoe String with you until get a job. So mote it be.

Psalm 119 v73-77

73 *Thy hands have made me and fashioned me: give me understanding, that I may learn thy commandments.*

74 *They that fear thee will be glad when they see me; because I have hoped in thy word.*

75 *I know, O LORD, that thy judgments are right, and that thou in faithfulness hast afflicted me.*

76 *Let, I pray thee, thy merciful kindness be for my comfort, according to thy word unto thy servant.*

77 *Let thy tender mercies come unto me, that I may live: for thy law is my delight.*

~~~~~~~~~~ *** ~~~~~~~~~~

Psalm 119 – Helping to understand and retain knowledge

Have a test or exam? Are you worried about remembering all those dates and details? Then use is working to help you absorb and keep all that knowledge you have learned. Also good for business & financial matters that must be remembered.

Day: Thursday pm
Incense: Lavender or Dragon's Blood
Herbal Tea-Blue Verbena (Vervain)-1/4 cup, Rosemary leaf-1/4 cup, Five Finger Grass-1/4 cup

Mix all herbs and store in an airtight container. Use 1 ½-2 teaspoons for a cup of tea. Let seep 4-6 minutes. Use honey to sweeten to taste. Drink daily when needed. Read verses of Psalm while drinking tea. Burn incense and drink tea during study sessions. So mote it be.

Psalm 119 v 9-16

9   *Wherewithal shall a young man cleanse his way? By taking heed thereto according to thy word.*

10 *With my whole heart have I sought thee: O let me not wander from thy commandments.*

11 *Thy word have I hid in mine heart, that I might not sin against thee.*

12 *Blessed art thou, O LORD: teach me thy statutes.*

13 *With my lips have I declared all the judgments of thy mouth.*

14 *I have rejoiced in the way of thy testimonies, as much as in all riches.*

15 *I will meditate in thy precepts, and have respect unto thy ways.*

16 *I will delight myself in thy statutes: I will not forget thy word.*

~~~~~~~~~~ *** ~~~~~~~~~~

Psalm 108 - Stopping someone from taking credit for your deeds

When others are taking credit for your work use this working to reveal the truth. Bring to light the matter and let all know that it was you.

Day: All
Incense: Dragon's Blood
Herb: Camomile Flowers-handful
Candle: Taper-Black
Other: Corn meal

Make a small circle using corn meal and Camomile flowers. Place candle in center of circle and light. Read verses of Psalm and burn incense. Sit in front of candle and repeat three times- 'The truth shall be for all to see. Let there be none to take credit for what I have done.' When finished pinch out candle and do not reuse. So mote it be.

Psalm 108 v 1-3-5-13

1   *O God, my heart is fixed; I will sing and give praise, even with my glory.*

3   *I will praise thee, O LORD, among the people: and I will sing praises unto thee among the nations.*

5   *Be thou exalted, O God, above the heavens: and thy glory above all the earth;*

13 *Through God we shall do valiantly: for he it is that shall tread down our enemies.*

~~~~~~~~~~ ******* ~~~~~~~~~~

Psalm 134 - Having success in college

Wanting to make sure you get the classes you want for the next semester? Do you want to have professors that will help you succeed? Use this working to help insure that things go your way while in college. Best to use at the start of every semester.

Day: All
Herb: Irish moss, Mugwort, Penny royal- equal amounts
Candle: Taper-Pink
Oil: Road Opener
Other: 7 shiny pennies, red cotton bag

Anoint self, candle and bag with oil while repeating verses several times. Light the candle and place pennies in a circle around it. Put herbs in bag. Place bag near candle. Once candle has completely burned out take pennies and put in bag. Place bag under foot of your mattress. So mote it be.

Psalm 134

1 *Behold, bless ye the LORD, all ye servants of the LORD, which by night stand in the house of the LORD.*

2 *Lift up your hands in the sanctuary, and bless the LORD.*

3 *The LORD that made heaven and earth bless thee out of Zion.*

Grimoires & Texts Referenced/Inspired By

"Sepher Ha-Razim/The Book of Mysteries" 3rd century, translated Michael A Morgan 1983

"Book of Raziel the Angel"13th century translated Steve Savedow 2000

"The Key of Solomon" 14th century, translated S. Liddell MacGregor Mathers 1888

"Heptameron" by Peter de Abano 1496- digital edition by Joseph H. Peterson 1998

"Three Books of Occult Philosophy" 16th century translated by Eric Perdue 2012

"The Book of Ceremonial Magic" by Arthur Edward Waite 1913

"6th & 7th Books of Moses" 1880

"Pow-wows" by George Hohman 1820

"Searching for Minerva," by Rob Oldham, *The South Magazine*, October/November 2008

"Root Doctors" by John J. Beck, *Encyclopedia of North Carolina*, edited by William S. Powell, 2006

'Mules and Men', Hurston, Zora Neale. HarperCollins, 2009.

"Magical Medical Practice in South Carolina.", Hawkins, John. Popular Science Monthly 70 (February 1907)

Hyatt, Harry Middleton. *Hoodoo – Conjuration – Witchcraft – Rootwork; Beliefs Accepted by Many Negroes and White Persons, These Being Orally Recorded Among Blacks and Whites*. 5 vols. Internet Archive has all volumes online: https://archive.org/details/HoodooConjurationWItchcraftRootwork

Websites

Biblecentre.org

Sacred-texts.com

Esotericarchives.com

Acknowledgements

This book would not have been possible without the generous support and wisdom of Papa Nico, Nico World Botanica. I came to learn about his magick and he taught me about my life. He showed me repeatedly that the impossible was possible. Through his shop doors many worlds were opened; forever changing what I thought I knew.

Thank you.

Keep your money safe, tell no one where you hide it & M.B. lady may this text be worthy of your wisdom. Amen said three times means "sumthen".

Thank you.

Stay in a state of service and you will always be receiving.

About the Author

Taren S stood in her first magickal circle at 17 years old in the back woods of North Carolina. She was initiated as a High Priestess (HPS) within American Witchcraft in 1995. Along the east coast, she has stood as HPS for main rituals at many large festivals and gatherings. In 2001, she stood as Raymond Buckland's High Priestess at GoddessFest, in New Orleans. At Phoenix Phyre'14 she was the HPS for the main ritual.

She has spent over 30 years living near the heart of Hoodoo country, Beaufort, South Carolina. Furthering her magickal and spiritual path she was initiated as a Mama Bridget within American Voodoo/Hoodoo in 2011. For over a decade, she has worked at a Haitian Voodoo Priest's botanica (shop) as a spiritual counselor and professional tarot card reader.

Currently, she lives in San Diego with her husband, three dogs and a black cat with an attitude.

My story

Someone once asked what made me spend many years researching and learning about hidden and forbidden knowledge in the Bible. The answer is really simple—my grandma told me a story.

By the flickering flame of a white candle and words spoken from the soul, she said the Bible could heal people and fix things. Neither Grandma's belief nor the image of her standing over a lit candle and intoning sacred words from the scriptures ever left me.

My paternal grandmother started me on a journey that, so far, has lasted over 35 years. It set my course for places I didn't know existed and learning that the impossible was indeed possible. I have traveled around this country and a few others all in search of the words.

Grandma was a pure Americana Southern Baptist prayer

healer from the Arkansas and Mississippi region. She went to church every Sunday and Wednesday. If someone had said to her anything about hoodoo or witchcraft, she would have run to the church with her hands in the air praying aloud. Her magick was strictly through the Word of God.

Grandma said she could feel things before they happened. One of her favorite stories to tell was that she knew the moment I was being born before anyone had called and to tell her. She told me it was because we shared a special bond.

She also spoke of being able to say holy words into a candle flame and heal people.

"What words?" I asked.

She smiled and said, "When you are older I will tell you."

Life twisted, and she never got that opportunity. I went on a quest to find the words, hidden in the Bible, that she spoke to help and to heal others. This book is a result of that journey, and I believe that somewhere in this text are words she would have spoken.

Thank you grandma, I love you and miss you. I honor your wisdom and pass it forward.

MOON

BOOKS

PAGANISM & SHAMANISM

What is Paganism? A religion, a spirituality, an alternative
belief system, nature worship? You can find support for all these
definitions (and many more) in dictionaries, encyclopaedias, and
text books of religion, but subscribe to any one and the truth will
evade you. Above all Paganism is a creative pursuit, an encounter
with reality, an exploration of meaning and an expression of the
soul. Druids, Heathens, Wiccans and others, all contribute their
insights and literary riches to the Pagan tradition. Moon Books
invites you to begin or to deepen your own encounter, right here,
right now.
If you have enjoyed this book, why not tell other readers by
posting a review on your preferred book site.

Recent bestsellers from Moon Books are:

Journey to the Dark Goddess
How to Return to Your Soul
Jane Meredith
Discover the powerful secrets of the Dark Goddess and
transform your depression, grief and pain into healing
and integration.
Paperback: 978-1-84694-677-6 ebook: 978-1-78099-223-5

Shamanic Reiki
Expanded Ways of Working with Universal Life Force Energy
Llyn Roberts, Robert Levy
Shamanism and Reiki are each powerful ways of healing; together,
their power multiplies. Shamanic Reiki introduces techniques to
help healers and Reiki practitioners tap ancient healing wisdom.
Paperback: 978-1-84694-037-8 ebook: 978-1-84694-650-9

Pagan Portals – The Awen Alone
Walking the Path of the Solitary Druid
Joanna van der Hoeven
An introductory guide for the solitary Druid, The Awen Alone
will accompany you as you explore, and seek out your own place
within the natural world.
Paperback: 978-1-78279-547-6 ebook: 978-1-78279-546-9

A Kitchen Witch's World of Magical Herbs & Plants
Rachel Patterson
A journey into the magical world of herbs and plants, filled with
magical uses, folklore, history and practical magic. By popular
writer, blogger and kitchen witch, Tansy Firedragon.
Paperback: 978-1-78279-621-3 ebook: 978-1-78279-620-6

Medicine for the Soul
The Complete Book of Shamanic Healing
Ross Heaven
All you will ever need to know about shamanic healing and how to
become your own shaman...
Paperback: 978-1-78099-419-2 ebook: 978-1-78099-420-8

Traditional Witchcraft for the Woods and Forests
A Witch's Guide to the Woodland with Guided Meditations and
Pathworking
Melusine Draco
A Witch's guide to walking alone in the woods, with guided
meditations and pathworking.
Paperback: 978-1-84694-803-9 ebook: 978-1-84694-804-6

Wild Earth, Wild Soul
A Manual for an Ecstatic Culture
Bill Pfeiffer
Imagine a nature-based culture so alive and so connected,
spreading like wildfire. This book is the first flame...
Paperback: 978-1-78099-187-0 ebook: 978-1-78099-188-7

Naming the Goddess
Trevor Greenfield
Naming the Goddess is written by over eighty adherents and
scholars of Goddess and Goddess Spirituality.
Paperback: 978-1-78279-476-9 ebook: 978-1-78279-475-2

Readers of ebooks can buy or view any of these bestsellers by clicking on the live link in the title. Most titles are published in paperback and as an ebook. Paperbacks are available in traditional bookshops. Both print and ebook formats are available online.

Find more titles and sign up to our readers' newsletter at
http://www.johnhuntpublishing.com/paganism
Follow us on Facebook at https://www.facebook.com/MoonBooks
and Twitter at https://twitter.com/MoonBooksJHP